GET STARTED QUILTING

GET STARTED QUILTING

The Complete Beginner Guide

Jessica Alexandrakis

INTERWEAVE.
interweave.com

Copyright © 2015 Quarto Inc.

interweavestore.com

Published in North America by
Interweave
4868 Innovation Drive
Fort Collins, CO 80525
www.interweave.com
All rights reserved.

Conceived, designed, and produced by
Quarto Publishing plc
The Old Brewery
6 Blundell Street
London N7 9BH

QUAR.LTQF

ISBN 978-1-63250-146-2

Senior Editor: Lily de Gatacre
Art Editor and Designer: Jackie Palmer
Copyeditor: Clare Sayer
Photographers: Nicki Dowey (lifestyle),
    Ned Witrogen (steps), Phil Wilkins (stills)
Illustrator: Kuo Kang Chen
Proofreader: Caroline West
Indexer: Helen Snaith
Art Assistant: Martina Calvio
Art Director: Caroline Guest

Creative Director: Moira Clinch
Publisher: Paul Carslake

Color separation in Singapore
    by Pica Digital Pte Limited
Printed in China by
    1010 Printing International Limited

10 9 8 7 6 5 4 3 2 1

For my grandmothers,
Frances Kampner and
Marion Hastings.

Contents

About this book

In the pages of this book, you'll find everything you need to get started quilting. You will be guided through the essentials of quilting, from fabric selection through to aftercare, before moving on to the comprehensive collection of quilting techniques. Including patchwork, appliqué, and improvisational techniques, there's something for everyone. In Chapter 3, you'll find a varied collection of projects that will inspire both beginner and seasoned quilters alike.

Chapter 1
Quilting Essentials
Pages 10–49

From choosing your fabrics, creating a quilting toolkit, and familiarizing yourself with your sewing machine, this chapter will give you all the information you need to start your quilting journey. Get to grips with the basics of English paper piecing and hand-appliqué, learn how to assemble your quilts, and find out how best to look after them once they're finished.

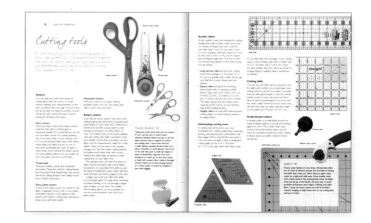

Mini quilts show you the effects you can create with your finished blocks.

Chapter 2
Quilting Techniques
Pages 50–127

Here you'll learn all the most important techniques, each one demonstrated on its own quilted block. You'll start with fundamental skills, such as sewing consistent seams on simple patchwork blocks, and gradually move to more advanced improvisational techniques and designs. Divided into patchwork, appliqué, and improv skills, you can dip in to learn a technique or create a block that particularly interests you, or work through slowly to develop a well-rounded quilting skillset.

All the tools and fabric you will need to complete this technique block are listed here.

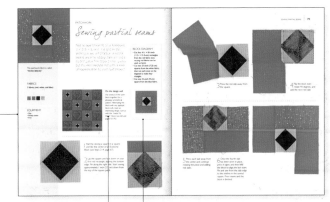

Want to use this block in a project? Here'll you'll find ideas for designs and other blocks to team it with.

Instructions for how to cut your fabrics and piece your block together can be found here.

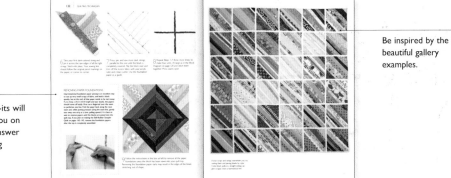

Be inspired by the beautiful gallery examples.

Tips and fix-its will help keep you on track and answer your quilting queries.

Chapter 3
Quilting Projects
Pages 128–149

Now it's time to put your newfound quilting skills into practice with these quilted projects. Use the techniques and block designs you mastered in Chapter 2, and follow the clear step-by-step photographs and instructions to create useful and beautiful items for your home.

Dimensions of the finished piece are detailed here.

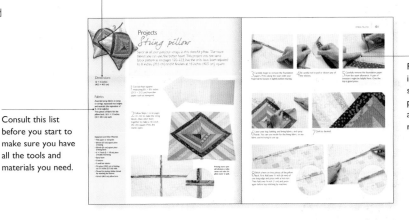

Consult this list before you start to make sure you have all the tools and materials you need.

Follow the clear instructions and step-by-step photographs to achieve amazing results.

Jessica's world of quilting

Quilting is not a new hobby, but it may be that you are a new quilter. Or perhaps you feel you are already a quilter, but you haven't actually made that many quilts yet. Either way, this book is for you. Quilting is for anyone and any time is a good time to start. No one is too old or too young, too busy or not artistic enough. This timeless hobby is both relaxing and exhilarating, private and social. It allows you to explore your creativity, and gives you an outlet to make things. Quilting is useful.

In quilt-making you are making something that may get passed down, saved, succeed you. The quilt you make this year may inspire someone else to start quilting in years to come. Quilts can bring comfort, give encouragement, or make someone's day, as well as making a room brighter. With color, shape, and pattern, you have the ability to influence the mood of your living space. Through your fabric choices, you are telling the world about yourself, or capturing memories to look back on. My own quilts reflect my experiences—quilts hand-pieced while traveling, made with fabrics gathered from friends. There are bee blocks, reconfigured UFOs, lots of improvisation peppered with inspiration found online and in my own home. To me, quilting is much more than just another way to fill your time and keep your hands busy. Quilting fulfills me, centers me, and helps me find my place in this world.

In this book you will find a collection of my favorite quilting techniques. I have chosen my favorite quilt blocks to teach you the craft of quilt-making and each block can be the stepping stone to a whole quilt itself. Some of them are traditional, some are trendy, some are my original designs. Each is set up to teach you one or more of the skills that you need to become a confident quilter. Once you learn the basic skills, you can try bending and breaking them. I'm not someone who likes to teach (or follow) all of the traditional quilting "rules." However, I do believe in solid construction. You want something that will last and that can be used; for this reason I'm not a fan of glues or embellishments. I like to make cozy, comfortable quilts that add decoration, change the mood of a room, and provide warmth and happiness.

My great grandmother made quilts and I grew up playing with her scraps (I remember she once let me thread her needle.) Both grandmothers were skilled with a needle—making curtains, clothing and housewares, but I learned to quilt from books, a few mentors, guilds, classes, and the online community. I encourage you to read all you can, find the methods that work for you, and get involved, either through your local fabric shop, quilt guild, or any of the number of websites where quilters gather. A list of online resources can be found at the back of this book.

Digital cameras, blogging, smartphones, and Instagram have become a big part of my quilting hobby over the years. I take progress shots of all my projects and share them on my blog and on social media. It's a great way to get feedback and nice to look back over a project once it's finished.

English paper piecing, hand-appliqué, and string piecing are some of my all-time favorite types of quilt construction. You've got to try a bunch before you figure out what clicks for you.

CHAPTER 1
Quilting Essentials

TOOLS & NOTIONS • SEWING MACHINE BASICS • ROTARY & FREEHAND CUTTING
FABRIC SELECTION • ESSENTIAL SKILLS • FINISHING & AFTERCARE

An introduction to quilting tools and notions

Quilts have been made for hundreds of years with little more than a needle and thread, some fabric and imagination. Thankfully, modern-day quilters have a lot of helpful tools and notions at their disposal to make the process easier and more enjoyable. Here are a few of the items quilters have come to "need" for their hobby. You don't need to rush out and buy each tool or notion on these pages, but, as you get more involved, this list will give you a good starting-point.

Fabric

Many people are first drawn to quilting because they fall in love with some fabric. Quilts can be made from all types of fabric, but when you're starting out, 100% quilt-weight cottons are best. They wash and wear well, and play nicely together. Cotton textiles come in a wide range of prints, solids, and nearly every color under the sun. Cotton fabrics can be beautiful, funky, or personal, as well as soft and inviting. If you don't have a stash started already, you'll need to get some fabric. Once you've made a few quilts and have a better feel for how fabrics behave when they are cut and sewn, you can branch out and try playing with voiles, corduroys, silks, denims, flannels, and upcycled clothing. For a detailed explanation on how to choose fabrics for quilting, turn to pages 20–27.

Batting

Batting is the soft layer that goes between a quilt top and the backing fabric. Battings can be made from cotton, bamboo, polyester, and even recycled plastic bottles. There are many brands of cotton or cotton/poly blends, but no matter what you choose, a low-loft batting, which is thinner and less fluffy, works best.

Straight pins

Straight pins are long and sharp, with a glass or plastic ball at one end. They are used to hold fabric patches together as you stitch by hand or machine. They come in a variety of thicknesses, so try out a few and see which you like best.

Pincushion

When piecing quilts, you will be moving between your cutting area, the sewing machine, and the ironing board fairly frequently. A nice sturdy pincushion will help you keep your straight pins off the floor and at hand when you need them. You can make your own or try out any of the store-bought pin holders available.

Needles

Machine-stitching: "universal" needles in sizes 10–12 (US) or 70–80 (Europe) are fine for piecing patchwork and assembling projects. Quilting needles are sharper and are designed to pierce through the layers of fabric and batting. Remember to change your needle at the beginning of each

new quilt you piece or machine-quilt. If you start working on several projects at once, get into the habit of changing needles every few weeks, depending on how much you sew.

Hand-stitching: when it comes to hand-piecing and appliqué, most quilters have their own personal preference. I like to piece and quilt with #10 Betweens, which are short and thick. For appliqué, sharps or straw needles are popular. Hand-quilting with Perle Cotton is easier with an embroidery needle. It is best to get a few different needles and see which ones feel more comfortable for you.

Thread

For machine-stitching, start with 100% cotton in a neutral color such as light gray or beige. If you are piecing patchwork in the same color family (i.e. reds and oranges), you can use a matching thread color. For handwork such as English paper piecing or appliqué, try to match your thread to your fabric color where possible. Hand-quilting thread is a little bit stiffer to prevent tangles. Perle Cotton #8 also works beautifully for big stitch hand-quilting. Threads for machine-quilting come in a wide variety of weights and styles. Try a few and ask other quilters what they use and soon you'll find which ones you like.

Seam ripper

Some quilters cringe when they think about seam

rippers, hoping they can avoid making mistakes in the first place but, the truth is, mistakes happen. They will be easier to fix if you have a seam ripper handy. Small plastic seam rippers come with most sewing machines, but fancy or ergonomic ones can make unstitching less of an unpleasant task.

Tape measure

Have a good tape measure in your sewing basket. A retractable one is fine, but if you get a long one (120 inches/3 m) made for quilters, you won't regret it. It definitely comes in handy when measuring quilt tops to add borders, sashing, or quilt backs and batting.

Rulers and templates

Acrylic quilting rulers have printed marks in a grid and when used together with a rotary cutter and self-healing cutting mat, these tools make cutting fabric a breeze. You can measure and cut accurate patches quickly and easily. Not all block units are squares, strips, or rectangles, though, and templates (which can be homemade from plastic or acrylic store-bought ones) come in handy to make a variety of block designs.

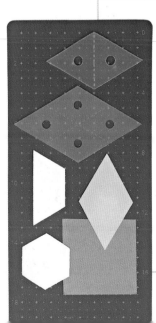

PAPER OR PLASTIC TEMPLATES

English paper piecing templates come in a variety of materials, but the most common are thin plastic or heavy paper (resources for both types can be found on page 154). With so much choice available, which should you use? Both types have their benefits— paper templates come in a wider variety of sizes and shapes, are relatively inexpensive, and can be easily folded to sew Y-seams. Plastic templates come at a higher cost but are far more durable. I have used the same set of 60-degree diamond templates to make three quilts! Plastic templates do not bend, though, so you must change your piecing sequence in order to be able to stitch Y-seams comfortably. I tend to use plastic templates for diamond patterns, and paper templates for everything else. Ultimately, it comes down to personal choice, so try out a few types and see what feels best for you. See pages 44–45 for more on English paper piecing.

Mechanical pencils or fabric marking pens

These are for marking sewing or cutting lines on your fabric as you piece blocks together. Fabric-marking pens come in many types—some erase with water, others disappear with heat. Make sure you read the instructions before using them, as some marking pen lines will become permanent if ironed!

Archival fabric-safe marking pen

These are for making quilt labels or adding signatures to your blocks for bees or friendship quilts. You will need to stabilize your fabric with some freezer paper before writing—see page 41 for more information on how to use.

Iron

To start, you don't need a fancy iron, just one with a cotton setting and steam/spray buttons. For safety, I like one with an automatic shut-off feature as well. After washing and drying fabrics, iron and fold them uniformly for easy storage. When piecing block units, press the seams to help the block lay flat and to make it easier to stitch units together smoothly. Be careful not to distort the finished quilt block by ironing too vigorously (moving the iron side to side while pressing). Some quilters advocate just pressing quilt blocks, which means to pick up the iron and set it on a seam, then remove it, without moving the iron as you apply pressure. I tend to be less fussy and have been known to "iron my blocks into submission" when a certain seam isn't perfectly straight or several fabrics meeting in a corner get a bit lumpy. Frustration is easily tempered with a hot iron. Many quilters also use pressing spray, which helps blocks lay flatter and makes them easier to piece together.

ADDITIONAL TOOLS

The following is a list of extra tools you may find useful when quilting.

HAND-SEWING TOOLS

- **Thimble**—hand-piecing, appliqué, and quilting are much more comfortable once you get used to wearing a thimble. There are many varieties available and it's best to test out a few different types until you find one that feels good on your finger.

- **Needle threader**—these small tools have a loop of wire at one end. Insert the wire in the eye of the needle, then pass your thread through the wire loop and pull the wire out again. Your needle is threaded without you having to strain your eyes.

- **Thread wax**—quilting wax is used to coat the thread to make it stronger as you hand-piece or quilt as thread can get worn and frayed from traveling repeatedly through the layers of fabric or from friction against the eye of the needle. Wax can also prevent thread from tangling. Run your thread over the wax before you start sewing to avoid frustration as you stitch.

- **Sewing kit**—if you like to take your handstitching with you away from home (at the doctor's office, quilt guild meetings, or on long journeys), it's a good idea to create a little sewing kit that can fit in your purse or bag. Plastic pencil cases or other small pouches work well and keep all your small tools and notions close at hand for when you've got the opportunity to stitch.

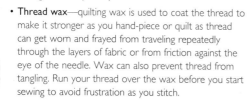

TOOLS FOR BASTING/QUILTING

- **Curved pins for quilting**—these are like safety pins with a curve in them and make pin-basting go much faster.

- **Kwik Klip**—this tool is used to close all the safety pins you used to baste your quilt. Not absolutely necessary, but it sure does save your fingernails.

- **Masking tape**—used to hold your quilt layers taut as you pin-baste.

- **Gardening gloves**—gloves with rubber fingers make it easier to grip and move your quilt for machine-quilting. You can purchase specialty quilting gloves at fabric stores, or use lightweight gardening gloves from home improvement stores.

ORGANIZING YOUR SEWING SPACE

If you are new to quilting and don't have a designated room in your house for this hobby, start by claiming a corner, shelf, drawer, or closet where you can keep your tools, notions, and fabrics safe and ready when you are. Latching plastic bins are great for storing notions and tools, and wall hooks keep scissors and rotary cutters safe and out of reach of curious little hands. Fabric can be stored in bins, drawers, on shelves, or in closets. It's best to keep your stash away from direct sunlight to prevent colors fading.

You will need somewhere to set up your sewing machine, as well as a designated spot for your cutting mat and a pressing station. For those of us tight on space, some quilt shops carry a dual cutting and pressing mat, which can really come in handy both at home and when traveling to quilt classes or retreats. If space is not an issue, don't forget to add bookshelves, a display of mini-quilts, some family photos, trinkets, a comfy chair, music, and a design wall!

Good lighting

Along with all the other tools we've gone over, it is very important to try to always sew with adequate lighting. When you set up your home sewing space, be sure to choose an area with lots of natural light, if possible, and if not, get a few good lamps. An OttLite, pictured here, or strong desk lamp at your worktable or over your shoulder will provide the extra light to see tiny stitches and thin threads. When you're off to a quilt retreat or guild meeting, be sure to pack a portable lamp in case the facility's lighting isn't ideal.

Make a design wall

Quilts can get big, and they look very different up close at the sewing machine to how they do spread on a bed or viewed from across the room. One way to help visualize a larger quilt during the design and piecing stage is to use a design wall. There are many ways to make one, but essentially you need a large area covered with a material that quilt blocks and fabric pieces will stick to without falling off. Felt-backed tablecloths, flannel sheets, and batting-covered foamcore are all good options. My design wall is made from a sheet of batting thrown over a curtain rod, mounted to the wall. I also have a smaller, temporary one made from a piece of batting with safety pins at the corners, which slips onto two hooks at the top of a closet door. I can throw up one block or audition fabrics for smaller parts of big quilts. For large quilts, or to see all the blocks together, it's nice to have a big design wall.

Cutting tools

So much of quilting starts with taking big pieces of fabric, cutting them up, and sewing them back together. The tools we use for cutting are important, specialized, and SHARP. Here we'll look at the different cutting tools available and their uses.

45-mm rotary cutter

Fabric scissors

Thread snips

Embroidery scissors

Scissors

You can make any quilt block design by cutting fabric with just scissors. It usually involves marking your measurements on the fabric somehow first (see page 33), but if they are all you have (or what you prefer), scissors will do the job in almost all cases. A good sewing kit will have a few types:

Fabric scissors

These are heavy, sharp, and usually pointed. Look for ones with a comfort grip or ergonomic handle. It is crucial that you do not use your fabric scissors for cutting anything else. If you have "help" in your sewing room or if you are sharing hobby space with others, clearly label your fabric scissors as such so they don't accidentally get used on paper or other things, which will dull the blades quickly. For most quilting cottons, you can usually cut up to two layers at a time comfortably.

Thread snips

These are smaller, pointy, and sometimes decorative. These are used for cutting thread, but if you don't have thread snips, any scissors will do for cutting threads, even safety scissors from a child's school box.

Sharp, pointy scissors

A pair of very sharp scissors are useful to snip fabric in appliqué. Scissors with a short blade, embroidery scissors, or the Japanese nigiri-basami work well for cutting seam allowances along curves and inner points.

All-purpose Scissors

These are useful to cut paper, batting, template plastic, trim, etc. Any heavy duty office scissors will work here.

Rotary cutters

Used with an acrylic quilter's ruler and a self-healing cutting mat, these tools revolutionized quilt-making. A razor-sharp disc is fitted into a handle and used like a pizza cutter to slice through several layers of cotton fabric at once. The marked lines on the acrylic quilting ruler and cutting mat make it possible to line up a straight cut and then accurately cut your fabric into the measurements called for in the pattern. Strips can be sub-cut into squares, triangles, etc. This tool makes cutting patches for quilting much faster than with scissors, without the added step of having to mark cutting lines on your fabric first.

The standard size is 45 mm. 4–6 layers of fabric can be cut cleanly with a fresh blade, but practice on scrap fabric first until you get the hang of holding the rotary cutter and how much pressure you need to apply to the ruler.

A larger size of 60 mm offers the ability to cut through layers of a quilt when trimming up before binding, or to cut through a larger stack of fabrics at one time. The smaller 28-mm blade allows you to accurately cut around curved templates with much less fabric waste.

TRAVEL SEWING TIP

Taking your hand work with you on a plane? It's ok—just be sure to check travel authority websites before you go to see the latest security rules in regards to scissors and cutting tools. I have never had any trouble taking a pendant thread cutter on a plane—domestic or international—but to be on the safe side, pack a small nail clipper or spool of dental floss separate from your sewing kit as a back up, in case your cutter or blunt kid's scissors don't make it through security. Never try to take sewing scissors or a rotary cutter on board an airplane in your hand luggage.

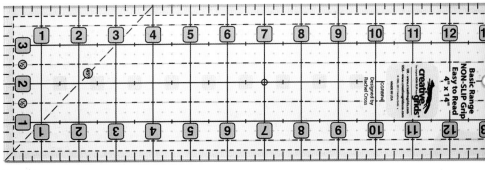

Long ruler

Acrylic rulers

Acrylic quilter's rulers are essential for cutting straight lines with a rotary cutter, and come in a variety of shapes and sizes. Look for one with clear 1-inch (2.5-cm) and ½-inch (1.3-cm) markings, with hash marks at ¼ inch (6 mm) and ⅛ inch (3 mm), and 45-degree and 60-degree angle lines. The sort of ruler you choose may depend on the type of task you are doing:

- **Long narrow rulers** are good for cutting strips from yardage. 6 × 24 inches (15 × 61 cm) is a popular size—make sure to get one that fits on your cutting mat (see below).
- **Square rulers** are good for trimming down block units or squaring up final blocks. Sizes such as 6½ inches (16.5 cm), 9 inches (23 cm), 12½ inches (31.5 cm), and 15 inches (38 cm) will come in handy. The large squares are also helpful when squaring up the corners of your finished quilt before adding binding.
- **Angled rulers** can help with measuring and cutting angles, or when lining up seams in an angled block.

Self-healing cutting mats

A cutting mat will become your new workstation for cutting, auditioning, measuring, pinning, and admiring your quilt blocks in all their stages. Find a mat that fits your space— if you are lucky enough to have a designated cutting table, go for a 24 × 36 inches (61 × 91.5 cm) mat, which will make it easy

to cut wide strips from yardage. If your sewing space is more limited, start with a smaller mat of 12 × 18 inches (30.5 × 45.5 cm). There are even smaller sizes too, which are great for bringing along to quilting classes, workshops, or retreats.

Cutting table

You can cut your fabric almost anywhere, but for safety and comfort, you should place your cutting mat on a sturdy, level table. If possible, find one with good height, so that the cutting surface comes to your waist and you don't have to bend uncomfortably as you slice with the rotary cutter. Home accessory stores may sell bed risers that can safely raise the height of your table by 6–8 inches (15–20.5 cm).

Small thread cutters

A thread cutter is a small blade encased in metal or plastic that you can pull your thread against to cut it. This is faster than using scissors, and some thread cutters can be worn as a pendant around your neck, making it always easily accessible—ideal for travel sewing kits.

Square ruler

Thread cutter

28-mm rotary cutter

Self-healing cutting mat

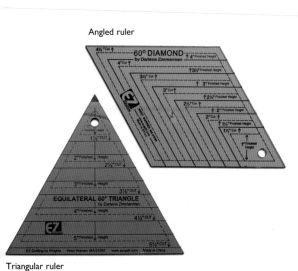

Angled ruler

Triangular ruler

SAFETY TIP

Rotary cutter blades are very sharp. Always keep them out of reach of children and get into the habit of closing the blade after every cut. Never leave an open rotary cutter on a table and walk away. Some models come with a safety feature that automatically closes the blade when you let go of the handle. Do your best to avoid accidents and protect your fingers, clothing, and other fabric. I keep my rotary cutters (as well as my fabric scissors) hanging on high hooks next to my cutting table, well out of reach.

Sewing machine basics

It may be that you've come to quilting after garment sewing for ages, or perhaps your first passion was knitting or crochet but now you're here, ready to work with small pieces of fabric and put them together into beautiful quilts. Either way, let's take some time to go over the basics of a sewing machine. There is a wide variety of sewing machines available to the home sewer, so the machine you have or use may not look exactly like the one shown here; however, all machines have the basic parts in about the same place. Let's have a look.

Needle (1)
Standard needles are best for quilting with cottons. Start with medium size (12/80.) Sewing machine needles have a flat back on their shank which fits into the hole of the machine. Tighten the screw by hand and then with the screwdriver that came with your machine. Refer to the owner's manual for instructions on how to change needles.

Presser foot (2)
The presser foot helps hold your fabric flat as you sew. Sewing machine feet can be changed out for various types of sewing (see page 20) and are attached with screws or clip-on mechanisms. There will be a lever toward the back of the machine (2a) that can raise and lower the presser foot, and some machines come with an attachment bar so the presser foot can be activated with your knee.

Throat plate (3)
This metal plate has a hole that allows the needle into the machine to catch the bobbin thread as well as slots, through which the feed dogs come up to grab the fabric. It usually has markings showing different spacings from the needle, allowing you to create accurate seam allowances. The standard patchwork seam allowance is ¼ inch (6 mm).

Feed dogs (4)
These metal teeth come through the bottom of the throat plate and grip the fabric, helping it move through the machine evenly as you sew. Most machines have a lever or switch, which allows the feed dogs to be "dropped" or lowered into the machine so they do not interfere with fabric movement. This is necessary for free-motion quilting.

Bobbin (5)
The bobbin holds the bottom thread, which when met with the top thread through the needle, forms the stitches that hold your patchwork together. Machines are either drop-in or front-loading. Drop-in bobbins get dropped into place through a plastic cover in the throat plate. Front-loaded bobbins must first be inserted into a round metal case and then a little arm is held out as the case is inserted into the machine. Bobbin casings should be cleaned of lint each time you change your bobbin.

Bobbin winder (6)
Usually the top of the sewing machine will have a little spindle to hold the empty bobbin and a marked path showing how to feed the thread from the spool, through a tension disc and onto the bobbin. Once the bobbin is in place and you are holding the thread end, slide the spindle toward the winder and either press the foot pedal or press the winding button. On basic machines, you may need to pull out the balance wheel to disengage the needle. Most bobbins will stop automatically when they are full.

Bobbin cover
On machines with drop-in bobbins, there is a plastic cover over the bobbin that fits into the throat plate. Front-loading machines have the bobbin case as part of the body of the machine, which must be opened to reveal the bobbin holder.

Threading path (7)
There is usually a clearly numbered path printed on the machine for how to guide the top thread from the spindle to the needle eye. Start by raising the presser foot to release the tension discs, then put your thread on the spindle at the top of the machine (7a). Make sure the thread is coming off the spool as indicated in the printed guide on your machine. If you have a flat disc that fits over the spool, slide it on the spindle. The thread then goes through a loop or hook, down and up through the tension discs, through a loop attached to the needle lift/lowering mechanism, before passing through a small bar at the top of the needle and then through the eye of the needle.

Thread cutter
Behind the needle to the left, you will most likely find a handy thread cutter. Computerized machines may have a thread cutting button which, when pressed, snips your threads and holds them inside the machine until you begin sewing again.

Needle threader (8)
Many sewing machines have an automatic needle threader. Operated by lowering a lever or pressing a button, it can help thread the eye of the needle quickly and easily.

Flat bed/free arm (9)
The flat bed is the area around the needle, which gives a flat surface to support your fabric. Some machines have a removable part of the bed exposing a free arm which is useful when topstitching bags and pouches, as well as sleeves or pant legs.

Stitch width and stitch length dials (10)
The stitch width dial allows you to choose the width of your stitches, as when making a zigzag. The stitch length dial adjusts the length from the top of the stitch to the bottom. The smaller the number, the smaller the stitch will be. For more on stitches, see page 21.

Stitch selector (11)

Even basic sewing machines are usually capable of sewing more than one stitch. Often the stitch choices are labeled with letters or numbers; you turn a selector dial or input the choice code (on computerized machines) to make your selection.

Tension dial (12)

Top thread tension is controlled by a numbered dial just above the needle area. When piecing patchwork, you shouldn't have to adjust the tension if your fabric weight doesn't change. If you are having tension issues, refer to Thread Tension Troubleshooting on page 21.

Reverse stitch lever (13)

Backstitches are used to "knot" your stitching at the beginning and end of seams. This is especially important when piecing patchwork as there are many points where the piece could become weak if the stitches are not secured. Your machine may have a lever or button. Press it and take a few backstitches; when you release the lever, the machine will sew forward again.

Balance/fly wheel (14)

The large wheel on the right-hand side of the machine is the balance wheel, which lowers and raises the needle one step at a time. If your machine doesn't automatically rest with the needle down when you remove your foot from the foot pedal, it is a good idea to get in the habit of turning the balance wheel to anchor the needle in the fabric should you need to stop or pause while stitching (for example, to remove pins or when sewing long seams.)

Foot pedal

On most machines, the speed of your stitches is controlled by how much pressure you apply to the foot pedal. The pedal will attach to your machine with its own cord, which is often retractable.

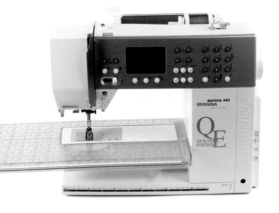

Some machines have extension tables that make a larger flat surface around the needle—especially helpful for machine-quilting.

Two threads, one from the spool at the top of the machine and the other from the bobbin, work together to form the machine stitch. The threaded needle passes through the layers of fabric down into the hole of the stitch plate. As it completes its journey to the lowest position and begins to move back up, a loop of top thread is formed. At that moment the bobbin shuttle rotates and the hook grabs the top loop and wraps it around the bobbin case, catching the bobbin thread. When the needle returns to its highest position, the threads should lock with one another in the middle of the fabric layers.

Zigzag foot

Sewing machine feet

Refer to your machine owner's manual for how to attach or remove feet. Always make sure to secure them tightly with the screw so they don't slip off or wobble while sewing. The following are the most commonly used sewing machine feet.

Zipper foot

Zigzag foot

This is the "regular" foot, or the one you will use for piecing patchwork, stitching on bindings, and assembling projects. It is used for all general sewing and does not need to be changed to complete the stitches below.

Zipper foot

While mainly used to insert zippers, this foot can also be used when adding piping and trim to household projects.

Walking foot

Walking foot

This rather large and bulky-looking foot will become your best friend once you start quilting. The walking foot feeds multiple layers of fabric and batting under the needle evenly so the top and bottom of your quilt don't shift as you sew. This reduces puckers and drag lines, and gives you more even quilting stitches. You can quilt straight lines, cross hatches, and even gradual wavy lines with a walking foot.

Free-motion foot/darning foot

A free-motion or darning foot does not clamp down on the quilt sandwich to keep it in place like the walking foot does. Instead, it hovers over the quilt, allowing you to guide the fabric in any direction to make curves, flowers, stars, and practically any quilt motif you want to try. The length of stitches is controlled by how fast you move your hands and press the foot pedal.

Free-motion/darning foot

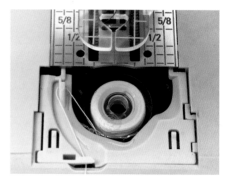

DROP-IN BOBBIN

This machine has a drop-in bobbin. The bobbin nestles in laying flat. Follow the instructions given in the owner's manual to thread the bobbin case correctly.

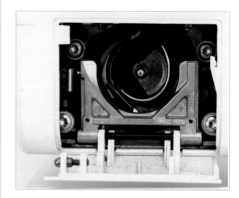

SET-IN BOBBIN

This machine uses a bobbin case to hold the bobbin. A door in the front of the machine arm opens to reveal the place to insert the bobbin case.

Stitches to know

Top

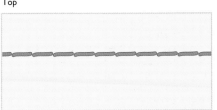

Straight stitch

This is the stitch you will use for all of your machine-piecing. A stitch length between 1.8 and 2.2 is normal for regular piecing. Foundation paper piecing requires a tighter stitch, between 1.5 and 1.6 will make it easier to tear off the papers in the end.

Top

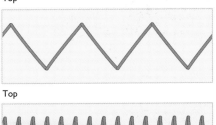

Top

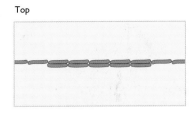

Zigzag

You won't often need to use the zigzag stitch while quilting, but it is useful for neatening raw edges of seam allowances (on the inside of pillow backs or bags, for example) and for joining batting scraps into a useable piece.

BACKSTITCH

Use the reverse stitch lever/button to take one or two stitches over the stitches you have just made. Do this at the beginning and end of each patchwork piece. When joining longer strips of patches, backstitch over each perpendicular thread that you cross.

Top

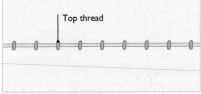

THREAD TENSION TROUBLESHOOTING

If your stitches don't look right, or if your patchwork seems loose and the patches can be easily pulled apart, you may have a problem with your tension. Often this can easily be resolved by rethreading the machine, or by making sure the top and bottom threads are being fed correctly (flip your spool over). If that doesn't fix it, see below.

Underside of fabric

Top thread

TOP THREAD LOOPS ON THE UNDERSIDE OF THE FABRIC

If the top thread gets pulled in loops on the underside of your fabric, your top thread tension needs to be adjusted. Start by stopping and rethreading your top thread. If the problem continues, slowly adjust the tension dial and sew a few stitches. Stop and check how they look and when they seem normal again you can continue.

Top side of fabric

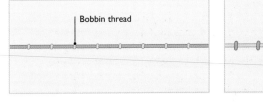

Bobbin thread

BOBBIN THREAD IS VISIBLE ON THE TOP FABRIC

If the bottom thread is visible on the top of your fabric, your top thread is too tight, forcing the bottom thread up. Slowly adjust the tension dial and check every few stitches until they seem normal again.

Underside of fabric

Top thread

TOP THREAD IS VISIBLE ON THE BOTTOM OF YOUR PIECE

If the top thread is visible on the bottom of your patchwork, the top thread may be too loose. Slowly adjust the tension dial and check every few stitches until they seem normal again.

Selecting and storing fabrics

A fabric stash is one of a quilter's most prized possessions. Keeping your fabrics organized and well maintained is important, but don't forget to shake them out and enjoy them once in a while. Shopping for, trading, sharing, petting, and appreciating fabric is a hobby in itself. Let's see what types of fabric are out there to make your collection glow and your quilts sing.

What fabrics can be used for quilting?

I stick with 100% cotton. Start there and once you feel more comfortable you may want to try out different fabrics. All the blocks and projects in this book are made with quilting cottons.

Where and how to buy fabric

Quilting cottons can be found in your local fabric store, from online quilt fabric stores, as well as from independent sellers on online marketplaces, such as Etsy. A list of my favorite shops is located in the Resources section at the back of this book. You can also try swapping or trading fabric in online quilt communities or through your local guilds. Some bed linen and even upcycled clothing can be suitable for the projects in this book.

How to stash, what and how much to buy?

It's easy to get carried away, but it's a good idea to start small, just buying what you like. Build your stash slowly—many shops sell bundles, so look for charm packs, layer cakes, and pre-cut bundles to help you get variety without having to buy yards of several different fabrics. After your first few projects, look at the fabrics left over from any bundles or sample packs that you bought. If you find you're avoiding a certain type or style of fabric, try not to stash that fabric in the future (even if it is on sale).

I am a stash quilter, which means I buy fabric I love when I see it and find ways to use it later. Very rarely will I choose the project first and then head to the fabric shop (maybe only for backing fabric). Bundles are a great way to get a variety of patterns in your stash, but don't rely on them too heavily. Anyone could have made that quilt with that one fabric collection, so how can we tell that it's yours? Spend some time at your local fabric shop just browsing to get a feel for what you like. There are many online resources for inspiration—Pinterest, Flickr, Instagram. Start collecting images of colors, textures, and patterns you love. Then when you go to buy fabric, you can build your stash with fabrics that you're more likely to use.

A friend posted an online fabric challenge last year—which are your favorite colors, and which are your true colors? I found that my true colors were the ones I felt most comfortable wearing, but my favorite colors were much bolder and brighter.

Pre-cut bundles are popular in fabric stores. They allow you to get a lot of variety and might expose you to fabrics you wouldn't have chosen on the bolt, but that you end up falling in love with.

I love the circles that float in the border of this Japanese quilt.

These leaves are the perfect color for a quilt I'm working on for a friend.

Patchwork pieced by my six year old. I'm inspired by his excitement and determined stitches.

Good luck charm

Seasonally appropriate moon-viewing stationery.

A mood board is a place to collect your ideas and help you remember your inspiration, places, quilts you want to make, and the people you want to make them for. I fill mine with anything that makes me happy.

The beginnings of a crumb block. One day I want to tackle an entire crumb quilt.

Use fabrics that are important to you and literally sew those good feelings into your quilt.

Choosing fabrics for your project

Most often I choose a palette, then sort through my stash and pull out anything in that palette. Then I step back and begin to weed things out. When I have narrowed it down to what I think I want to work with, I'll leave the pile there for a day or two and see if my mood changes. I might make some changes, but if I still like it after a few days, then I know I've got something good.

The fabric in a quilt can add movement, mood, memory, and meaning. Because I buy fabrics I love, it's easy to influence the mood of a quilt by including a fabric that has special meaning for me. For example, I backed a quilt I made for my mother with a white print with tiny blue birds (see left), so now, whenever I add leftovers of that fabric to another project, I feel the memory of my mother, both as I work on the project and when I use it after it's complete.

Background fabrics

Neutral fabrics

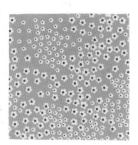

Low-volume fabrics

What is a background fabric?

Background fabric is traditionally the main fabric in a quilt, acting as a backdrop so that the focus fabrics and block pattern can jump forward. While in many quilts, both traditional and modern, this fabric is light-colored, it doesn't necessarily have to be. Beautiful quilts have been made with red backgrounds, small prints, or many different light-colored fabrics (now sometimes called low-volume, see below).

What is a neutral fabric?

Neutral is a fabric that acts as a resting place for your eyes. It does not necessarily need to be a light color, a solid, or even the main background fabric of your quilt. It just has to be a fabric that unifies your design in some way, and allows there to be a thread of calm through the work.

What is a low-volume fabric?

Low-volume is a term that has come to describe a range of fabrics that might include neutrals, solids, or patterned fabrics that "read" as light-colored. When used together, these fabrics form a neutral background and a varied and interesting place of calm in your design. Many fabrics can fall into the low-volume category, but they must play nicely together and blend in when you step back from the quilt, squint, or take off your glasses. They should read as one value.

Background fabric

Neutral fabric

The large expanse of pale background fabric means that the star motifs really pop on this neutrally colored quilt.

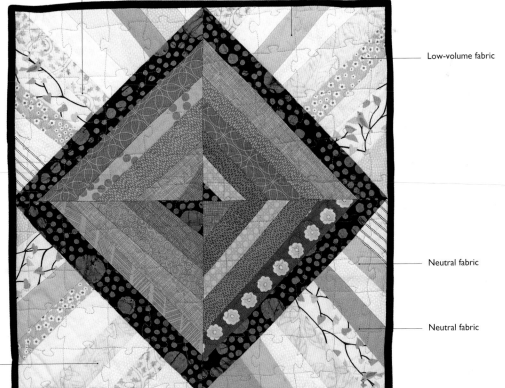

Low-volume fabric

Neutral fabric

Low-volume fabric

The neutral and low-volume fabrics in this pillow case work together to create a design that is tonally calm despite it using numerous fabrics, colors, and patterns.

Neutral fabric

Neutral fabric

Low-volume fabric

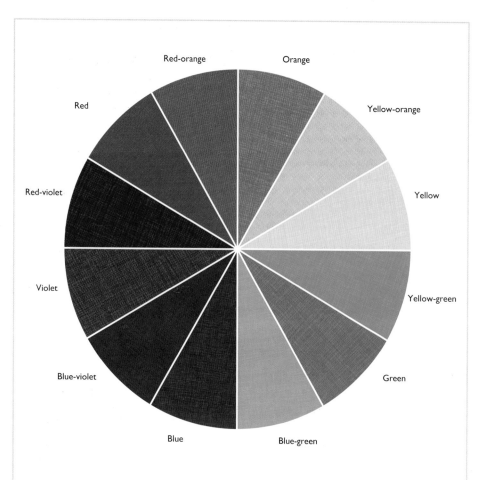

Contrast

When you are choosing fabrics to go next to each other in a quilt block or overall design, contrast is an element that can't be ignored. Color, value, shade, and hue can all influence the way a pattern "reads" when it is sewn into a quilt.

Overall, the fabric you choose to put into your quilt will take on a life of its own as it settles in next to its new friends. Here I feel very strongly that breaking the rules and trusting your intuition is necessary. Make quilts with fabrics that you love. Feel free to mix up collections and genres— batiks with solids, reproductions with modern prints. Fifty years from now, they'll all be "old" fabrics anyway. Let the quilt historians of the future scratch their heads and marvel at your creativity.

This is a good example of bold contrast. All units of the block are made by combining a dark fabric with a light fabric.

Fabrics of a similar hue or value can blend in together and help a secondary pattern become visible.

If there is not enough contrast between fabrics, the overall pattern can get lost.

YOUR INDISPENSABLE COLOR TOOL

Colors can be visualized in a circle or "wheel." There are numerous ways of dividing this wheel and using it to mix and match your fabrics.

- Primary colors are red, yellow, and blue. They are pure colors—not made by mixing other colors—and are bold and bright.
- Secondary colors are orange, green, and violet, made by mixing adjacent primary colors. Yellow and red make orange, yellow and blue make green, and blue and red make violet.
- Tertiary colors are made by mixing adjacent primary and secondary colors. For example, red (primary) and orange (secondary) will create red-orange. The tertiaries extend one color into another.

- Analogous colors are any three adjacent colors on the wheel, such as blue, blue-violet, and violet. These combinations have a calm, harmonious effect.
- Complementary colors are opposite each other on the wheel, such as blue and orange. They make each other appear more intense and vivid.
- Triadic colors are at the corners of an equilateral triangle overlaid on the wheel, such as red, yellow, and blue or orange, green, and violet.
- Quadratic colors are colors at the corners of a square or rectangle overlaid on the wheel, such as red-violet, orange, yellow-green, and blue.

TESTING YOUR PALETTE

When you think you have your palette, cut a swatch of the fabrics you want to use and sew them into a strip. Carry this strip with you and use it to audition additional fabrics from your stash, your friends' stashes, or at the quilt shop. This way, you'll be able to select fabrics that you know will go with what you already have. This tip is also useful when stitching English paper piecing projects like the Doll Quilt on pages 146–149. In that example, I used a strip to help remember where I wanted each fabric to go.

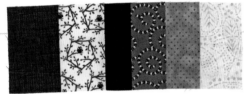

Can I combine prints?

Yes! Of course you can. Quilts can be made from just one fabric, and two color quilts are striking, but I am of the mind that the more fabrics you use, the merrier. Some quilts end up on the wall or in a gallery, but most live out their lives on the bed or couch, keeping someone warm. I like to give that person something to do, something to look at, something to look for. Combining prints gives a lot of visual interest, and it's a great way to show off your stash. Before you start cutting the fabrics you'd like to use, open them up and see how they read. Stand across the room and squint, take a digital photo and view it on your phone/camera, or my favorite tactic—take off your glasses. Now you can see if the fabric reads as one color, as a light or a dark, or if the print has some aspect that makes it stand out more than you had originally thought. Here are a few things to keep in mind when choosing your prints:

Scale

Pay attention to scale

Depending on the size of the print motifs, you may choose to use some fabrics in certain ways. A medium to large print makes a good focus fabric or border. A small or tiny print can be used as a background. When you cut up a large print fabric into 2½-inch (6.5-cm) squares, the motif may be lost entirely, or the fabric won't read as the color you had originally thought.

Direction

Pay attention to direction

Some prints have an obvious top and bottom. You can either choose to cut and place these carefully, so that all the trees are going the right way, for example, or you can let the patches fall as they will. Stripes can make interesting secondary patterns when you pay attention to cutting, joining, and fabric placement. Play around and see what you like best.

Intensity

Pay attention to intensity

Some prints can be bold and intense, while others are more subtle. Prints with contrasting colors or novelty designs can add interest or detract attention from your overall quilt design, so choose carefully.

CHOOSING THE RIGHT PRINTS FOR *BRODERIE PERSE*

Any fabric can be appliquéd onto a background piece to create an image, but using patterned fabrics in appliqué allows the fabric to dictate more of the design. On pages 100–101 you will learn the technique of Broderie Perse, or appliqué with patterned fabric. Here are some examples of some fabrics that may work well:

Cut out leaves, but be sure that you have left enough seam allowance to be able to see the design.

Too much background fabric on your appliqué piece may break the flow of your overall design.

Pictures on different colored backgrounds can add or detract from your overall design. If the image is too small, it may get lost.

PREWASHING

When you get your fabric home from the store, open it up, shake it out, and toss it in the washing machine. Wash on a cold water cycle with a gentle detergent. I recommend prewashing all of your fabric, even scraps that have been gifted, found, purchased, or reclaimed. I wash all my fabric, even pre-cuts, because if I don't, I may run into the problem of not knowing what has been washed and what hasn't. For yardage, I like to snip the corners off with scissors before washing a length of fabric. This cuts down on excess threads getting tangled and later it helps me remember what was washed and what wasn't.

Use lingerie bags for your small scraps (anything smaller than a fat quarter) and toss them in with other larger pieces of fabric. I always wash fabric separately from clothes and other household laundry and I always throw in one or two color catchers or dye cloths that absorb excess dye from the wash water. Sort into lights and darks and wash bold colors like reds and purples separately. I dry large pieces of fabric in the dryer on medium heat, or hang them on a drying rack. If you toss scraps into the dryer, you'll end up with wrinkled confetti! I still do this, but if I want to save the hassle of ironing all those little pieces, I will lay out wet scraps on a bath towel to dry overnight.

Storing your fabric

Collecting beautiful fabrics is all very well but if you haven't worked out how to store them effectively, you will soon run into difficulties. I once knew a quilter who had taken over the walk-in closet in her master bedroom for her stash. Who needs to look at clothing when you've got fabric to store?

When choosing how to store your fabric, keep in mind that if you can see it, you are more likely to use it. If you can't see it, you may forget you have it and end up buying more of the same thing. Open shelving and clear plastic bins are great for this reason. However, it is important to note that prolonged exposure to sunlight can fade and damage fabric, so if your stash is in a room that gets a lot of natural light, you might want to consider covering it with a curtain or something else to protect it. Cabinets with solid doors, closets, or drawers may work better for you.

I would love to share my secrets for a perfectly maintained stash, but the truth is, my fabric is stacked in piles and baskets around my sewing room. Many times I can't find what I'm looking for, but the process of digging and searching often leads to fabric combination discoveries that I wouldn't have come up with otherwise.

How to sort

One thing that I am good at is sorting scraps. If you love the look of scrap quilts and can feel yourself wanting to make one, then hold on to them. Get a bin to keep near your cutting table to collect small pieces, and a larger bin under the table to collect larger cutoffs (or to dump the smaller bin into when it gets full). Clear plastic bins or drawers in assorted sizes work very well for keeping small bits of fabric organized. While some quilters prefer to sort by color, I sort mine by size and potential future use—crumbs, squares, strings, strips, and chunks. That way, if I need a certain size scrap, I can just pull my "short strips" bin and start off on some string pieced blocks. If I'm looking to make a test block or a small project, I'll start in the "less than a fat quarter" bin and try to use up something that would otherwise get passed over. I tend to save my yardage for bigger projects and piecing quilt backings.

Sorting is also a personal preference. If you find you prefer to make projects from one designer's collection, then keeping those fabrics together instead of separating them out by color would probably work best for you. I have my fabrics sorted by cool and warm colors (there's a blue, green, and purple bin, and a neutrals, browns, and black bin), with separate piles for solids, novelties, and holiday prints. The main thing to consider is to stick with an organizational method that works for you. If you can't find it, you can't use it.

How to cut

Let's get cutting. All of the techniques and projects in this book have cutting instructions, usually indicating how many patches to cut in each fabric, and to what size. For the machine-pieced blocks, these are mostly cut with a rotary cutter. For the appliqué or improv blocks, scissors may be necessary. Let's start with the anatomy of a cut of fabric (see right).

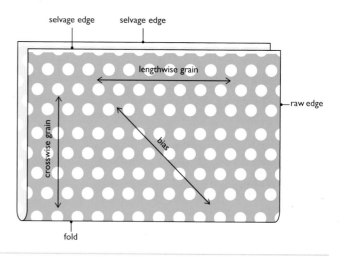

selvage edge   selvage edge

lengthwise grain

crosswise grain

bias

raw edge

fold

Ripping fabric

Sometimes purchased fabric yardage will be cut with a rotary cutter and the cut edge will not align with the straight of grain. If this bothers you (not all quilters pay attention to grain lines), you can straighten up the edge following these instructions.

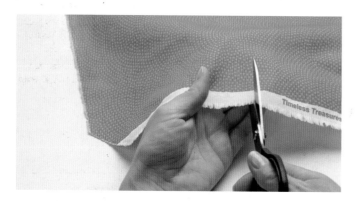

1 Begin by making a small snip with scissors a few inches in from the cut edge, and ripping the fabric.

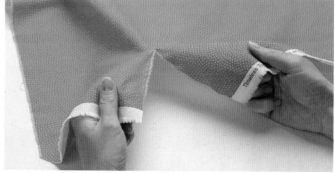

2 It will rip along the grain line and then you know your patches will be straight. When using a large piece of yardage for a quilt back or borders, it is also easier to rip off the selvage edges in a similar manner.

3 After ripping fabric, press the ripped edge to smooth out the warps and ripples. The fabric edge has been abused, though, and may never lie flat. Sometimes this can be hidden in the seam allowance of future blocks, but if it bothers you, use your rotary cutter to trim off between ¼ and ½ inch (between 6 mm and 1.3 cm).

Rotary cutting

Rotary cutting can be more accurate and faster than cutting patches with scissors. Give yourself a head start toward easy cutting and make sure to iron your fabric flat before you start.

Cutting strips

I Place a length of fabric on your cutting mat and lay your ruler on top. Follow the lines of the ruler with your eyes to be sure the fabric is lined up correctly underneath before you make your first cut. Place the rotary cutter against the ruler's edge, press firmly and evenly, and cut away from you.

2 You can also rotary-cut the selvage off, and cut long strips with your acrylic ruler by first folding the fabric and aligning the edges with your ruler lines. With a sharp rotary blade, you should be able to cut through six layers at a time as shown here.

Cutting squares and rectangles

Cut strips into squares and rectangles by aligning the ruler in the same way as before, and cutting across the strip of fabric.

Cutting triangles

Cut a square in the usual way, then line up the 45-degree angle on the ruler with the edge of the square and cut along one diagonal to make a half-square triangle. Cut again for quarter-square triangles (see right).

Using templates

Straight-sided shapes can be cut using templates and a ruler for perfectly straight edges. Pin the template to the fabric with flat-headed or small-headed pins. Place the ruler ¼ inch (6 mm) away from the edge of the template and cut.

Cutting borders and sashing

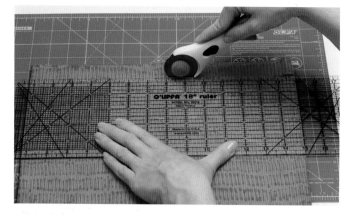

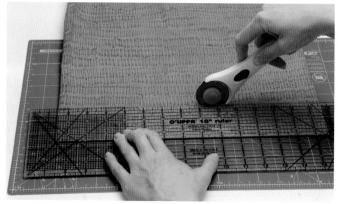

1 A rotary cutter can be used to cut borders or sashing along the selvage edge, from one piece of yardage. Fold the fabric carefully after washing and pressing, making sure it will fit on your cutting mat. Cut off the selvage.

2 Flip the fabric and cut off the width of strip you want.

FUSSY CUTTING

Careful cutting of prints to highlight a certain motif or design is called "fussy cutting." This technique can add a lot of visual interest or surprise in otherwise simple blocks, or can take a complex pattern to a higher level.

Trimming up blocks

Appliqué and improv blocks need to be trimmed square before they can be added to a sampler quilt, such as the one on pages 142–145.

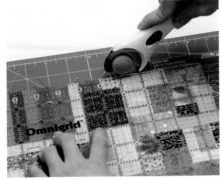

1 To do this, start by placing the pressed block on your cutting mat. Use a large square ruler to line up two edges, and trim.

2 Flip the block and align the trimmed corner with the marked lines on the ruler.

3 Trim the final two sides in the same way and you have a square.

Cutting with scissors

Scissors are used in quilting to cut patches and appliqué shapes as shown at right.

Curved pieces for patchwork and appliqué can also be cut with a rotary cutter. Use a small cutter (a 45-mm blade), place the edge next to the curved acrylic template, and cut. If you are working with curved paper templates, it is better to transfer them to double-thickness, quilting-template plastic, or stick with scissors.

1 Trace around a template with a fabric-marking pencil.

2 Pin the template to the fabric and carefully cut around it.

CUTTING CONTINUOUS APPLIQUÉ

When cutting continuous appliqué (for example for Hawaiian—see pages 96–99 or Ainu—see pages 110–111 work), pin the template to fabric or trace it with a fabric-marking pencil, then cut out with scissors.

Assembling and finishing

Once your pile of blocks has grown or your project top is complete, it's time to learn how to put it all together and make it into a quilt. On the following eight pages you will find general guidelines and instructions for putting your entire quilt together. These tips and instructions will work for any bed quilt or smaller quilted project. As with everything in the craft of quilt-making, there are many ways to get the job done—if your favored method differs from this guide, please do whatever works best for you.

Top: This quilt has thin sashing with corner stones, or squares of contrasting fabric where the sashing intersects.

Bottom: This quilt does not have sashing. Instead, the large half-square triangles are sewn directly to each other. This creates a lovely secondary pattern of blue and orange diamonds.

Joining blocks

After making a pile of quilt blocks, you must decide how to join them. The first decision to make is "to sash or not to sash." Sashing is thin strips of fabric that are sewn between the blocks to separate them and frame them a bit within the quilt. The width or color of the sashing can change the look of a quilt completely.

Joining without sashing

If you don't want to sash your blocks, square them up to the finished size, pin them right sides together, and assemble them in rows. Press all the seams in a row in one direction, and the seams of the next row in the opposite direction. Pin the two rows right sides together, butting seams, and assemble the quilt blocks into a top.

Sashing your blocks

If you feel the quilt would benefit from sashing, first decide how wide you'd like it to be. If you have a short stack of blocks but want to make a big quilt, sashing is a quick way to add inches to your project. Cut vertical sashing strips into your chosen width multiplied by the unfinished length of your blocks, for example 3½ × 12½ inches (9 × 31.5 cm), for 3-inch (7.5-cm) finished sashing and 12-inch (30.5-cm) finished blocks. Pin the sashing strips to the blocks and join them into rows as indicated in the illustration. Between rows, cut horizontal sashing strips to the length of the measurement of the width of the rows, after vertical sashing has been included. Join the rows with sashing in between.

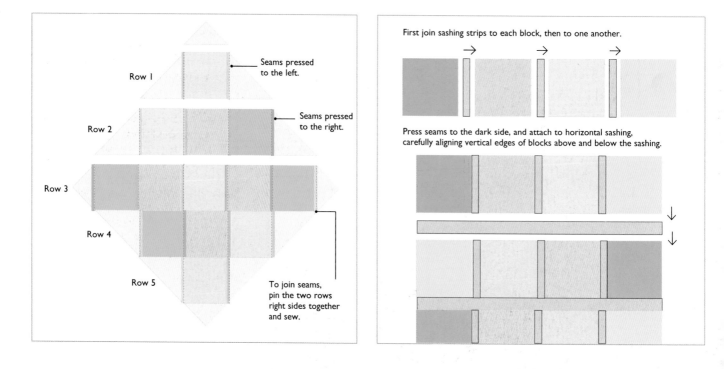

Row 1 — Seams pressed to the left.

Row 2 — Seams pressed to the right.

Row 3

Row 4

Row 5

To join seams, pin the two rows right sides together and sew.

First join sashing strips to each block, then to one another.

Press seams to the dark side, and attach to horizontal sashing, carefully aligning vertical edges of blocks above and below the sashing.

Borders

Borders are strips of fabric that go around the outer perimeter of your quilt, framing the design. They can be pieced or solid lengths of fabric. A quilt can have one or two borders, or none at all—it's all up to the quilter to decide as he or she designs and creates his or her piece. To create a simple border treatment, add two vertical borders on either side of the top, and border pieces to the top and bottom of the quilt (see pages 143–144). Measuring border pieces can be tricky because not all quilts end up the exact size the maker intended. Before attaching your borders, follow the guidelines below to cut them accurately.

- To avoid wavy borders, measure your quilt through the center, vertically. This is the length of the vertical border strips. After adding the vertical borders, measure the quilt again through the center, horizontally. This is the length to cut the top and bottom borders.
- When adding border strips, first find the center of the border by folding it in half and marking with a pin, pinching, etc. Find the center of the edge of the quilt top. Match these two markings and pin outward toward the edges. Do this for all four border units.

Pressing

Before quilting your top on your home machine or sending it to a long-arm quilter, you must press the finished patchwork carefully.

- A good press makes sure that the quilt top is flat and does not have any creases. It also flattens the quilt out to its actual size.
- As you press, make sure that the seams fall in the direction you had planned.
- Take time during this step to remove any stray threads or fuzz from your quilt top, especially on the underside because you don't want an errant dark thread peeking through your beautifully pieced white quilt top.

Backing fabric

The underside of the quilt is usually made from a single piece of fabric wider than the quilt top.

- Extra-wide backing fabric (108–120 inches/275–300 cm) is available from some fabric stores and many online retailers.
- You can piece your backing from yardage or an assortment of large pieces of fabric. Be sure to remove selvages from the stitched edges and piece your backing with a ½-inch (1-cm) seam allowance. Pieced backings have become quite popular as an added design element to quilts and many great examples can be found on blogs and photo-sharing sites such as Flickr or Pinterest.

- If you are going to be sending your quilt out to a long-arm quilter, be sure to check with them about how to prepare your quilt top and how large your batting and backing need to be in relation to the size of your quilt.

Batting

There are many options for batting types, but, whichever you choose, a low-loft batting works best for hand- or machine-quilting. Purchase a piece of batting that is roughly 4 inches (10 cm) bigger than your quilt top on all sides, and keep in mind that most battings will shrink once the quilt is washed. Many quilters like the soft and wrinkled effect this gives, but if you would like to avoid it, batting can be prewashed. See the manufacturer's instructions.

GET SOME HELP

Layering and basting your quilt can be backbreaking work. Why not invite a friend to help you out? A second set of eyes can help make sure your layers are straight, and a second pair of hands will make the job go faster.

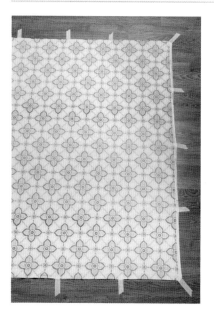

1 Start by laying your backing fabric face down on a wide, flat surface. Depending on the size of your quilt top, you may be able to do this on a large table or else on the floor.

2 Using masking tape, tape your backing fabric to the floor or table at the edges. Start with the top and bottom center, then do the sides and then the corners. Be sure that the fabric is taut but not distorted. Continue to tape around the edges until the backing is secure.

3 Lay your batting on top of your backing and carefully spread it out, being sure to flatten any wrinkles. You should be able to see 1 inch (2.5 cm) of backing fabric all around the edge. Tape it down in a few places to hold it securely.

4 Lay your quilt top on top, right side up. Leave 2–4 inches (5–10 cm) of batting all around the edges. Smooth it out with your hands and tape it in place at the edges, in the same way that you taped down the backing, taping opposite edges to ensure that it is taut but not distorted.

Basting

Quilts can be basted in three ways: with spray baste (adhesive), with thread, or with curved quilter's safety pins. The method you choose will be determined by the size of your project, how you plan to quilt it, and your personal preference.

- **Spray baste** works well for smaller projects, such as the Doll Quilt and Pillow (see pages 146–149).
- **Thread-basting** is popular if you plan on hand-quilting, since the quilt can then easily be manipulated and moved around in a large or small quilting frame or hoop.
- **Pin-basting** is fast and effective, and very convenient if you plan to quilt by machine. This is the method we will use here.

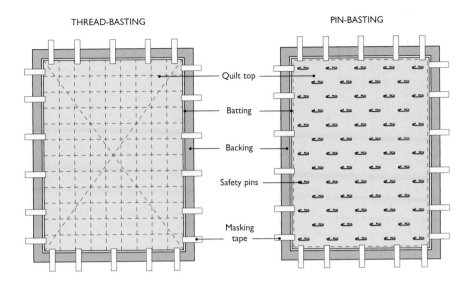

THREAD-BASTING

PIN-BASTING

Quilt top

Batting

Backing

Safety pins

Masking tape

Whether you choose to baste with thread or pins, be sure to baste the three layers securely to avoid them shifting as you quilt, which can result in puckers on your finished quilt.

WARNING!

Basting with safety pins may scratch or damage the floor or tabletop where you have laid out your project. It is best to find a suitable surface on which to baste, such as laminate tiling or an area that you won't mind scratching.

5 Starting in the center of your quilt, insert safety pins, being careful to collect all three layers before you bring the pin up again.

6 Place your pins 5–6 inches (13–15 cm) apart across the top of your quilt, working in quadrants. There are specialty tools sold at quilting and fabric shops that can assist in closing the pins and saving your fingernails. If you can't find one, a spoon should do the trick.

7 Place a few extra pins all along the outer edge of your quilt top to keep it securely basted.

Quilting

Quilting stitches are what keep the three layers of the quilt together, making it a "quilt." You can put these stitches in yourself by hand or machine, or hire someone else to do it for you. When you quilt your quilt yourself, the three layers must be basted together first (see pages 36–37) so that they don't shift as you stitch. When you send your quilt to a professional long-arm quilter, you send the three layers separately and the quilter will load them onto her machine (wrapping them around long polls) and then unwrapping them as she progresses with the quilting. Examples of the most popular types of quilting are shown below. Hand-quilting with thin thread (traditional hand-quilting) is very popular. Though any thread can be used, special hand-quilting threads are available which have been coated with wax to give them strength and help you stitch through the layers of a quilt more easily. Hand-quilting thread may feel "wiry" when coming off the spool.

PREPPING QUILTS FOR LONG-ARMING

So you want to send your quilt out? Professional long-arm quilters provide services to piece backing, baste, quilt, make and attach binding, and even finish quilts all for a fee. You can find long-arm quilters by asking around at your local guild or fabric store, browsing quilts at a local show, or asking other quilters in an online community. When choosing a long-armer, first try to see some examples of their work—many have websites, blogs, or photo galleries online. Next, contact the quilter and discuss what you would like to have done.

Discuss payment, postage (for out-of-town quilters), and preparation—how much backing and batting fabric to send, how to label the top of your quilt top, etc. Also—price. Usually this will be a price per inch, varying on the amount of detail or "custom" work you want applied. Make sure to explain how the quilt will be used (see pages 46–47 for some good descriptions). Some quilters prefer to do pantographs (repeated rows of design), while others do free-motion or computer-guided quilting. Try to share (in person or by email) examples of designs you like and ask if they can do the same.

Hand-quilting with perle cotton

Perle Cotton #8 is a good-sized thread to use for hand-quilting when you want the quilt stitches to demand attention. The larger stitch length necessitated with the thicker thread also means the quilting can be completed faster than with traditional hand-quilting thread.

Machine-quilting with a walking foot

You can pin, baste, and machine-quilt straight or wavy lines with the walking foot on your sewing machine. The walking foot, along with the feed dogs, controls the layers of your quilt so that the stitches come out evenly.

Machine free-motion quilting

To make curved or other designs with your quilting stitches, a free-motion or darning foot is necessary. With free-motion quilting, you move the quilt sandwich under the needle to create the design. The stitch length is controlled by how fast you move your hands and how hard you press the presser foot. It may take some practice in order for your stitches to look the way you'd like, but it's well worth the effort. Free-motion quilting is an art form in itself.

Long-arm quilting

Long-arm machine-quilting services have become popular over the last few years. Most quilters don't have space for the large quilting frame at home, but you can send your quilt to a professional quilter if you don't want to do it yourself.

Bias binding

To cover the edges of the quilt, you will need to make double-fold bias binding. To find out how much binding you will need, measure the four sides of your quilt, add them together, and add 12 inches (30 cm).

1 Begin by cutting strips 2¼ inches (5.5 cm) wide on the 45-degree angle of your fabric. Join the strips on the diagonal with a ¼-inch (6-mm) seam, and trim the excess fabric. Fold the strip in half lengthwise and press, wrapping the bias tape around a small board or other handy tool to prevent it getting tangled.

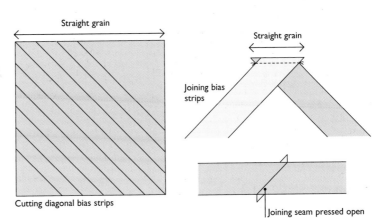

Straight grain

Cutting diagonal bias strips

Straight grain

Joining bias strips

Joining seam pressed open

2 When you are ready to attach the binding, first open the edge and fold in about ¼ inch (6 mm) of fabric. Press.

3 Start about 8–10 inches (20–25 cm) down from one corner of your quilt and pin the raw edge of the binding to the front of your quilt, aligning the edges.

4 Continue pinning until you come to a corner. Insert a pin through the binding and your quilt at a 45-degree angle, toward the corner of the quilt. Then pull the binding up and fold it at that angle before folding it down on itself and along the next edge of the quilt.

5 Continue pinning the binding along the edges of the quilt, repeating Step 4 at every corner.

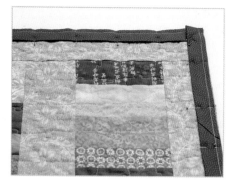

6 When you reach your starting-point, overlap the binding by about 1½ inches (4 cm). Then open the binding strip and cut it at a 45-degree angle.

7 Open the starting point of your binding, carefully tuck the end into the beginning, and pin in place.

8 Machine-stitch the binding on with a ¼-inch (6-mm) seam.

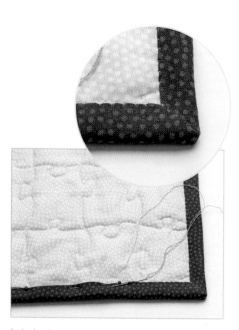

9 When you come to each corner, fold the flap out of the way and stitch to within ¼ inch (6 mm) of the edge. Backstitch here to secure the corner. Then release the presser foot and, without cutting the threads, turn your quilt so you are ready to sew the next side. Fold the binding flap back into place and stitch over it as you come down the new side, backstitching at the start to secure your corner point. When you come to the end of your binding, backstitch again to secure the threads before cutting them.

10 Fold the binding around to the back of your quilt and secure it with 5–6 straight pins. The binding fabric should cover the stitching line from Step 8. Begin whipstitching the binding to the backing of your quilt, taking care not to let any stitches show on the front.

11 At the corners, fold the binding in along one side, creating a 45-degree angle at the edge. Then fold it back onto itself along the next side, creating a mitered look. Secure the corner with a few backstitches as you continue to whipstitch around the edge.

Labels

Quilts are a part of our material culture and have the possibility of becoming family heirlooms or being bought and sold as pieces of art. Therefore, it is very important that you attach a label to each quilt you make. Labels can document who made the quilt, who it was made for, where it was made, and if it came from a published pattern or from the quilter's own design.

Sunshine & Shadows
made with love by,
Jessica Alexandrakis
Westbury, NY
2014-2015

1 To make a quilt label, you will need a light-colored fabric, a piece of freezer paper (with a plastic coating on one side), and a fabric-safe pen or marker.

2 Begin by ironing the coated side of the freezer paper to the wrong side of your label. This will stabilize the fabric so that you can write on it.

3 Document your quilt's information with a fabric-safe pen. Consider including: the name of the quilt, your name, when and where it was made, who it was made for, your inspiration, information about the fabrics, and care instructions (particularly if it is a gift).

4 Add any additional decorations you'd like, such as rubber-stamped images with fabric-safe permanent ink. Remove the freezer paper and press the label from the wrong side to heat-set the ink.

5 Fold in ¼ inch (6 mm) on all sides and press the seams. Pin the label in place on the back of your quilt and attach it with a whipstitch.

Hanging sleeves

You may want to hang up your quilts to display them, at home or at a quilt show. In which case you'll need to add a hanging sleeve. There are many ways to do this—here are a few options for you to consider:

• Create a tube from a length of fabric 8½ inches (21.5 cm) high by the width of your quilt minus 5 inches (12.5cm). Fold in short sides twice, press, and topstitch. Fold in half the long way and pin into place along the top edge of the quilt. Attach binding by machine to the front of the quilt, catching the sleeve edge at the same time. Fold over the binding and finish as usual, then pin and stitch the bottom edge of the sleeve to the back side of the quilt by hand. Be careful that your stitches don't go through to the front.

• When the quilt is already bound and you put on a sleeve as an afterthought. There are two options:
- Make a tube as described at left, but pin it upside down, just under the binding. Then sew a line from the right side of the quilt, just below the binding (stitch in the ditch), securing the hanging sleeve. Flip over the quilt, fold down the sleeve, and press with a hot iron. Pin into place and sew down by hand with a whipstitch.

- Make a tube by sewing along the long edge on the machine, then folding the tube to hide the seam at the back. Pin the tube in place at the back of the quilt and whipstitch both the top and bottom edges. This is especially useful on very large quilts (king sized) because you can make two shorter tubes with a gap in the middle, in case the quilt show or gallery people need to add an extra hook along the pole to support the weight of the quilt. Also, some shows require that quilts hang so many inches from the floor so a sleeve like this can be positioned at a specific measurement, not necessarily at the top of the quilt.

Hand-stitching

Sewing with a machine is an excellent skill to have but don't shy away from hand-stitching. Over the next few pages we'll look at the basics of hand-appliqué and English paper piecing, techniques which can make your quilt-making more portable and relaxing. Learning these skills will give your projects a truly unique unique and hand-crafted quality. You can see further techniques that utilize these skills on pages 88–105.

Hand-appliqué basics

Appliqué is when one or more fabrics are layered on a background and the seam allowance is turned under and stitched, either ahead of time or as you work. As well as being very relaxing to do—and portable— hand-appliqué can give a beautiful, personal look to your projects. The five blocks on pages 88–105 each teach a different appliqué style, from Hawaiian appliqué to Broderie Perse. Once you've had a go at the basic skills, practice on these blocks and watch your quilting repertoire soar.

Things to note
Thread choice

I like to use 100% cotton thread in a color similar or a shade lighter than the fabric being appliquéd. In multi-fabric designs, change the thread colors if possible to match each patch. Some quilters like silk threads or very lightweight threads. Experiment to see what works best for you.

Needles

I may be in the minority, but I do all my appliqué with a #10 quilting Between needle. This short, thick, sharp needle is usually preferred for hand-quilting, but I tend to use it for everything. There are longer needles with a thin shaft called sharps or straw needles that many quilters prefer for hand-appliqué. Again, experiment and see what feels best in your hand.

Thimbles

You will get a lot more enjoyment from hand-appliqué if you can get used to wearing a thimble. Try one on the middle finger of your stitching hand, and use it to push the needle through the fabric layers. If it feels awkward at first, give it time or switch to a different style of thimble. The extra hours you will be able to stitch are far more valuable than the amount of time spent getting used to wearing one, so don't give up!

Let's appliqué
Centering your design

First cut a background square. All the appliqué blocks in this book call for a square to be cut ½ inch (1 cm) larger than the finished block. This allows for some neatening up if the fabric edges fray or if the appliqué causes the edges to get distorted as you sew. Fold the block in half and press with a hot iron, making a crease. Fold in half again and iron again, creating four quarters. This will help you center your design on your background.

Basting

Use a contrasting thread color so as not to confuse it with your stitching thread. Take long stitches through all the layers. Don't knot at the beginning and end, just backstitch. Stitch about ½–¾ inch (1–2 cm) away from where your appliqué line will be. Once your appliqué block has been securely thread-basted, you can bunch the block up in your non-stitching hand and take stitches with your dominant hand.

How to hand-appliqué

Start by knotting the end of a single strand of cotton thread, 12–18 inches (30–45 cm) long.

Bury your knot behind where you plan to start stitching. If possible, try to secure your knot in the seam allowance of the appliqué itself. Bring the needle up on the edge of the appliqué piece and take your first stitch straight down into the background fabric. Bring the needle up through the background and the appliqué fabric and repeat. Every three stitches or so, hold the thumb of your non-stitching hand over the most recent stitches and pull your thread taut to tighten the stitches and make them "melt" into the fabric.

Whipstitching a pressed appliqué piece

A few of the appliqué blocks you will create in this book use patches that have already been basted or otherwise pressed (see "Dresden Plate," pages 88–91, "English Paper Pieced Hexagon Star," pages 102–105, and "Mixed-Technique Basket," pages 124–127). This means that you are not working with a raw edge when you stitch them to the background fabric. As such, they may be good ones to start with to get comfortable with taking appliqué stitches, using the technique described here, as you won't have to worry about fraying edges or even seam allowances.

Needleturn appliqué

The remaining appliqué blocks in the book use the needleturn technique. Here an appliqué shape is cut out and basted to the background fabric. The raw edges are visible and seam allowances are not marked. The needle is used to gradually tuck under a seam allowance as you whipstitch the motif to the background fabric. See the panel at right for more information about the needleturn technique.

Bias lines

One way to get thin lines of appliqué is to make "vines" of fabric cut on the bias. First cut a strip of fabric along the bias, about 1¼ inches (3 cm) wide. Line up the 45-degree mark of your acrylic ruler with one straight edge of the fabric and cut across. When fabric is cut on the bias, it stretches easily, which we can use to our design advantage. Fold the

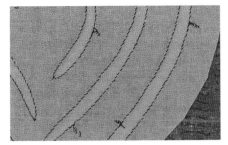

Thread tail buried under extra stitches at the back of your appliqué.

strip in half, wrong sides together and press. Pin in place and stitch with a ¼-inch (6-mm) seam by hand or machine. Remove the pins and fold the vine over the seam allowance. Press and whipstitch into place.

Stopping and continuing your thread
When you near the end of your thread or have come to the end of your stitching, take a stitch and pull the thread and needle to the reverse of the piece. Flip it over in your lap (or on a table) and take three small stitches in the background fabric only, underneath the appliqué piece. Then take your needle and run it under those stitches, burying your thread securely under them. Then snip the thread. If you need to continue with a new thread, knot it and bury it in the seam allowance a few stitches back from where you left off. Then take the first stitches with the new thread over the last stitches you had taken.

Pressing
Remove the pins and basting stitches. Press the block from the back, face down on the ironing board and be gentle.

Squaring up a block
After you have pressed your finished block, take it back to the cutting table and, using a square acrylic ruler, align two edges and trim. Then rotate the block, line up the freshly cut corner with the ruler marks of your unfinished block size, then trim up the remaining sides (see page 33).

Needleturn appliqué
Let's look in more detail at how to appliqué using the needleturn technique. Instead of having the entire seam allowance pressed under before stitching, here only one inch or less is turned under at a time, allowing for a smooth rhythm of stitches and folding as you follow the raw edge. Special care needs to be taken for points and valleys to insure that the seam allowance gets folded under smoothly.

1 Pin the appliqué in several places and thread-baste to the background with long stitches and basting thread. Your basting stitches should be ½–¾ inch (1.3–2 cm) from the raw edge of the motif fabric.

2 Begin to needleturn appliqué by burying your knotted thread in the back of the flower fabric, then turning down ⅛ inch (3 mm) of the raw edge and whipstitching it to the background. Use the tip of the needle to slide the fabric under itself. Use the side of the needle to glide along the top of the fold to crease a sewing line.

3 When you come to a point in your motif, such as a petal or leaf, stop stitching about ¼ inch (6 mm) from the edge. Make an extra stitch where you want the point to end, then use the needle to sweep the seam allowance under the point you have just stitched. Pull the thread gently to make the fabric pop into a point. Continue turning the seam allowance under with the needle as you sew down the next side.

4 When you find a "valley" in your motif, like the bottom of the petals in this Hawaiian pattern, sew up until ½ inch (1.3 cm) away from the valley. Slide the needle into the valley and swipe the seam allowance to one side. Do not turn under the bottom of the "V." Instead, make three deep stitches into the flower fabric before sweeping the seam allowance up and under on the other side.

The basics of English paper piecing

English paper piecing (EPP) is a patchwork technique where fabric is sewn around paper templates to keep the shape and then whipstitched together to create a geometric pattern. Once the seams are joined, the templates are removed and can be reused.

Attaching fabric to templates

| Place a template into the center of the wrong side of your fabric.

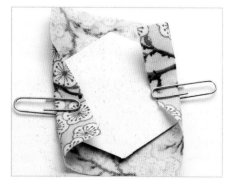

2 Baste the fabric to the paper template by folding the fabric over and securing with two paper clips.

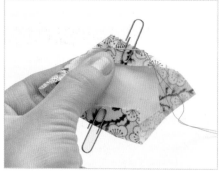

3 Knot the basting thread, fold over the first corner and take a backstitch (two stitches in the same spot), catching the fold.

4 Fold over the next corner and take another backstitch. Continue until all corners are secure. Repeat for all the templates.

Joining templates

| Join the templates with a whipstitch. Start by burying the knot in the seam allowance and taking a few stitches to secure it, coming up at the corner where you will start to sew.

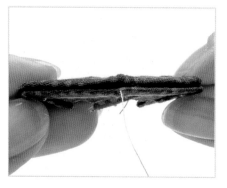

2 Place two templates right sides together, aligning all the corners.

3 Take a stitch into the corner of the second template and back through the first then pull securely.

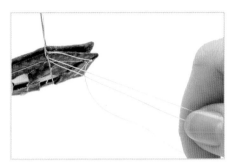

4 Take another stitch in the same spot, this time wrapping the thread around the needle before pulling through to make a small knot at the corner (this is known as a "wrap knot").

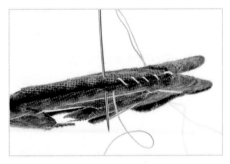

5 Begin to stitch from corner to corner, taking small bites of fabric along the edge of the template. Do not sew through the template paper. Instead, use the template as a guide to slide the needle along as you take each stitch.

6 When you reach the end of the template, take an extra stitch and slip the needle through the thread to knot it.

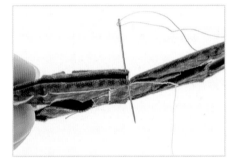

7 To join another template, leave the thread as it is, open the first two templates and place a new one along the seam you plan to sew. Take two stitches in the same spot of the corner and again make a wrap knot to secure it.

8 Stitch to the next corner as before and finish with a wrap knot in the corner. Next, travel with the thread along the seam allowance and back to the corner of the templates to be joined.

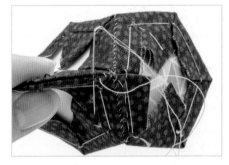

9 Fold the piece to align the corners to be sewn. Whipstitch to the next corner.

10 To end a line of stitching, make a wrap knot, take three stitches back over what you have just sewn, and bury the thread by working it into the seam allowance.

REMOVING TEMPLATES

After all the edges of a template have been sewn, remove it by reaching in with your fingernail or a crochet hook, grasping an edge, and pulling it out. There is no need to remove the basting stitches.

Caring for your quilts

Now that you have made a quilt, what should you do with it? How do you make it part of your life and what do you need to know about taking care of it? Everyone is different—here's a bit of insight into what I do, but, as always, do what works best for you and your family.

Washing and drying

I wash my quilts in a number of different ways based on which of the following categories they fall into:

Daily-use family quilts

These are the quilts that stay in steady rotation on beds and on the family room sofa. The ones I don't mind getting turned into play forts, dragged around the house, tossed in the car for road trips. The ones that have seen food spills, grimy fingers, silly putty, and baby spit up. They have been through the bed wetting phase and carsickness—made with love and used with love. I know these won't last forever and, like childhood, I want to enjoy them while we can.

- Machine-wash warm, normal cycle.
- Tumble dry medium.
- I use the same detergent and fabric softener as I do for our family clothing.
- I wash them when they get dirty, sometimes as often as twice a month. Frequent washings will wear them out faster, which is why I have lots (8 currently, for my family of 4) and use them in rotation.

Good quilts

These may get put on beds or on the back of the front room sofa, but the kids know better than to play with them. My washing suggestions are below but if the quilt is hand-pieced or hand-appliquéd, you may want to hand-wash it.

- Machine-wash cold, normal or gentle cycle.
- Tumble dry low or hang to dry.
- I use the same detergent and softener as our family clothing, but use your discretion. If you'd rather use a delicate detergent, do so.
- I wash these as infrequently as possible, maybe once a year unless accidents happen.

Display quilts

These are the quilts that hang on the wall or are made for quilt shows, and are intended for display only. No cuddling.

- Depending on the method of construction, machine- or hand-wash cold.
- Hang to dry.
- Gentle detergent.
- Wash as infrequently as possible. I have some quilts in this category that have never been washed at all.

How to hand-wash a quilt

Fill a large tub, washtub, or your bathtub with cold water. Add gentle detergent and agitate with your hand before adding the quilt. Unfold the quilt and let it slide into the tub. Use your hands to make sure all areas of the quilt are wet, then gently begin moving the areas of the quilt up and down to force the soapy water through the layers. Let the quilt soak for ten minutes. Gently squeeze the quilt and rub the fabric together to try to release any stains. Drain the soapy water and refill the tub with clean water. Agitate the quilt gently with your hands, trying to force clear water through the layers. Drain and refill, repeating this process until the water stays clear (no bubbles) while you're agitating it. Drain the tub one last time and press down on the quilt to squeeze out as much water as you can. Don't wring the quilt. Lay some towels down on the floor and spread the wet quilt on top of them. Layer with more dry towels and starting at one end, roll the quilt/towel sandwich onto itself so that the towels absorb the water from the quilt. Unroll and hang to dry on a sturdy laundry line, out of direct sunlight if possible.

Hints and tips

PROTECT THOSE COLORS

The first time a quilt is washed, I toss in a few Color Catchers dye cloths which absorb excess dye from the wash water and stop it from bleeding onto other areas of the quilt. To be extra safe, take care to prewash your fabric before starting to sew.

Using

I like to make quilts that can be used. On a bed or sofa, cuddling under a quilt is hands down better than making do with a store-bought blanket. When your quilt is being cuddled, let it be loved! When it's not, it will look lovely folded and laid across the back of the couch, chair, or on the foot of the bed (assuming the bed is made with another quilt already). Try not to leave your quilts in direct sunlight or outdoors for extended periods of time (for example, in the back of the car, forgotten on the laundry line) as light can fade and weaken the fabrics. If you have pets, I'm sure they'll want to cozy up to your quilts as well, just take care to remove pet hair as needed.

Hanging

Some quilts were made for display. If your display quilt is large, consider adding a hanging sleeve (see page 41) and hanging it from a curtain rod installed on an empty wall. Quilts can also be hung from rods using several curtain clips. If the quilt is smaller (under 30 inches/76 cm), binder clips and removable hooks are my preferred hanging method.

Storing

When you aren't using your quilts, there are several ways you can store them:

- Quilt racks are a nice way to keep family quilts close at hand in case someone gets cold, or to keep them in the room during the warm months when they're not needed all the time. You can find them commercially or have some custom made. Quilt ladders make a nice conversation piece.
- Chests or decorative cabinets can keep them out of the way and dust free.
- In closets, quilts can be stored folded in clean pillowcases and stacked on shelves. This is the best method for long-term storage. Remember to take them out every year or so and refold them on different lines so that they don't get permanent creases along fold lines.
- If you don't have closet space, try layering them on unused beds, just make sure to rotate the pile so the one on top doesn't get too much damage from sunlight.

REPAIRING QUILTS

Quilts get worn with use; that is part of their beauty. If well-loved quilts start to show wear and you'd like to make small repairs, see if these tips can help. Please note that these tips are for making repairs to your own contemporary quilts, at your own discretion. This advice is not intended as instructions on how to restore old or antique quilts.

REPLACING A WORN BINDING

There are two ways you can do this. Option A is to carefully cut off the old binding, including up to ½ inch (1.3 cm) of the actual quilt edge. Do this with a rotary cutter, acrylic ruler, and a cutting mat. Make a new binding and stitch it on by machine, finishing by hand (see pages 39–40). This option will give you a less bulky edge, but the look and size of the quilt will be altered, depending on whether or not it had a border.

Option B is to cover the worn binding with a new, slightly wider binding. Make a new binding slightly wider than the original (2¾-inch/7-cm wide strips, if your original was 2¼ inches/5.5 cm, for example). Pin and sew it in place using a ⅜ inch or ½ inch (1 cm or 1.3 cm) seam allowance. Flip and stitch down by hand.

REPAIRING WORN OR FRAYED PATCHES

Appliqué shapes over any worn spots by pinning cut fabric onto the quilt and using the needleturn method (see pages 42–43) to appliqué it down. Depending on the size of the worn spot/patch, you may want to add additional quilting stitches through the new patch to hold the layers together. It is nearly impossible to completely hide this type of repair; instead, allow it to add character to the quilt and extend its life.

REPAIRING SPLIT SEAMS

If the stitches between patches have come undone, thread a needle, tie a knot, bury it in the quilt layers, and then use whipstitch or ladder stitch (which is less visible than a whipstitch) to join the patches again. This takes patience, but it is worth it to stop the batting from peeking through.

REPAIRING WORN QUILTING STITCHES

If hand- or machine-quilting stitches have come loose or undone, lay the quilt out somewhere flat and mark out the repair quilting pattern/design with water-soluble marker (or just do it free hand). Then, get your hand-quilting supplies or sewing machine and go over the loose or broken stitches. If it is a relatively small area, the rest of the quilt should stabilize the three layers as you repair them. If the area is larger than 12 inches (30.5 cm) or so, first baste with thread or pins to stop the layers from shifting as you quilt.

GIFTING

If you decide to make a quilt as a gift, it is important to give the recipient some information about the quilt and its future care. The first thing to do is to make and attach a label (see page 41) so that anyone who sees or uses the quilt later on knows where and when it was made. It is also sweet to include whom it was made for and any event information ("made for Janel and Ted to celebrate their wedding") or other wishes you would like to share. Then include a card with the quilt, detailing washing and drying instructions. The baby quilt you gift will have a higher chance of being used if new parents know that it can be just thrown in the washer. No one wants a gift quilt to end up at the back of a closet.

CHAPTER 2
Quilting Techniques

BASIC SKILLS • PATCHWORK • ENGLISH PAPER PIECING • HAND-APPLIQUÉ
IMPROVISATIONAL TECHNIQUES • MIXED TECHNIQUE BLOCKS

This patchwork block is called
"RAIL FENCE"

FABRICS

8 fabrics ranging from light
to dark.

EQUIPMENT

- Acrylic ruler
- Rotary cutter
- Pins
- Iron

Sewing a consistent quarter-inch seam

A ¼-inch (6-mm) seam is essential for most machine-stitched patchwork. It is the standard seam allowance in quilt patterns and books, and being able to sew one consistently is one of the first skills a quilter needs to acquire. It is easy to start and end with a ¼-inch (6-mm) seam, but keeping it consistent along the length of your fabric takes some practice. This block allows you to work on stitching long seams with a ¼-inch (6-mm) seam allowance so you can get comfortable with them before moving on to more complex blocks.

BLOCK DIAGRAM
Cut two strips 2 × 13½ inches
(5 × 34.5 cm) from each fabric.

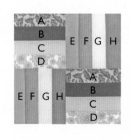

On the design wall

Identical blocks placed in a straight setting gives the appearance of basketweave. Try combining with "Granny Square" (see below right and pages 68–69), "Hawaiian Appliqué Block" (see pages 96–99), or "Inside My Heart" (see pages 92–94).

1 | Start by placing two strips (A and B) right sides together. Align all the edges and pin. Stitch a ¼-inch (6-mm) seam, backstitching at the beginning and end.

2 Open out the two strips and press with a hot iron. Measure the unit; it should be exactly 3½ inches (9 cm) wide.

3 Align strip B with a third strip (C) and pin. Stitch together, carefully maintaining a ¼-inch (6-mm) seam from beginning to end. Open the strips and press with a hot iron. Measure the unit; it should now be exactly 5 inches (12.5 cm). Add the fourth strip in the same manner, then press and measure as before. The strip set should be exactly 6½ inches (16.5 cm) wide.

Hints and tips

ROOM FOR ERROR

When sewing strips into "strip sets" which will be sub-cut later, it's always a good idea to cut your strips a little longer than you actually need, giving yourself some wiggle room in case the edges don't match up perfectly at each end. In this block, we cut strip sets into 6½-inch squares, so instead of cutting our individual strips 2 × 13 inches (5 × 33 cm), we will cut them 13½ inches (34.5 cm) long and trim off the excess.

A fat quarter bundle can really go far with this pattern. Make a bunch of identical blocks and the dark and light fabrics will be evenly distributed across your top.

4 Repeat Steps 1–3 to make a separate strip set using four different fabric strips (E–H).

5 Cut each of your strip sets in half into two 6½-inch (16.5-cm) squares.

6 Stitch two different squares together, rotating one of them 90-degrees as shown, and using a ¼-inch (6-mm) seam as before. Stitch together, open, and press.

7 Repeat with a second pair of squares and then stitch together. Your block is finished and you've mastered the ¼-inch (6-mm) seam.

This patchwork block is called
"TRIP AROUND THE WORLD"

FABRICS

7 fabrics ranging from light to dark.

EQUIPMENT

- Acrylic ruler
- Rotary cutter
- Pins
- Iron

Chain piecing

Chain piecing is the technique of sewing several units at one time, without cutting the thread in between. This skill is useful as it helps increase speed when piecing, making an assembly line of the patchwork. Often when sewing patchwork by machine, there are a lot of squares or units that need to be joined in a certain order. By creating this block, you will learn how to chain piece parts of the block, and then keep the rows of the block connected as you join them. This trick prevents accidental shuffling of patches and keeps your patchwork on track.

BLOCK DIAGRAM

Cut 2½-inch (6.5-cm) squares from the seven different colored fabrics as follows (see diagram):
1 × A, 4 × B, 8 × C, 10 × D, 8 × E, 4 × F, 1 × G.

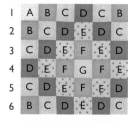

Row						
1	A	B	C	D	C	B
2	B	C	D	E	D	C
3	C	D	E	F	E	D
4	D	E	F	G	F	E
5	C	D	E	F	E	D
6	B	C	D	E	D	C

On the design wall

Play around with the block layout and see what types of pattern appear. Depending on where you place light and dark fabrics, portions of the design recede or pop. Try combining with "54–40 or Fight" (see pages 74–77).

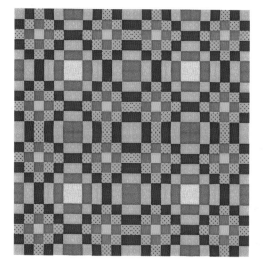

1 Lay out all 36 squares next to your sewing machine, following the Block Diagram (left). Take a picture with your phone or digital camera to help you remember the layout. Starting at the top right, stitch two squares right sides together, backstitching at the beginning and end.

2 Then, leaving the thread intact, pick up and stitch the next two squares in the second row. You will have a tiny chain of thread between the pieces of fabric.

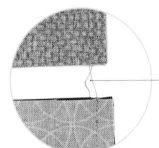

Leave the thread intact between squares to create your "chain."

3 Continue until the first pair of squares in each row are joined, then cut the thread. Take the third square from the top row, match it to the top piece in the chain and stitch. Without cutting the thread, attach all of the third column. Repeat until all the columns are attached. You will have six rows with chains in between.

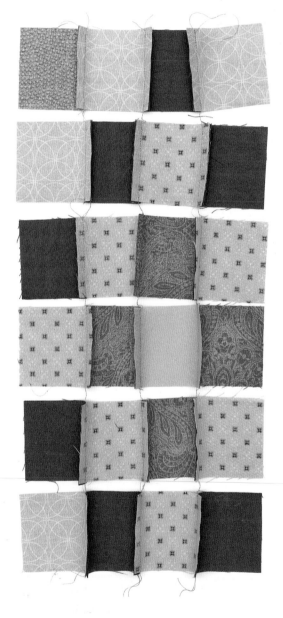

Fix-it

BUTTING UP SEAMS

When joining portions of a quilt block, it is very common to press seam allowances in opposite directions and then butt them up against each other before sewing the cross seam. This technique of butting up seams serves a few purposes. First, by fitting your fabrics together this way and then pinning at the seams as they butt together, it helps keep your block in line as you assemble units or rows. If you don't butt up your seams and pin before sewing, your corners or points may be "off" and not match up. For blocks that rely on block intersections to form a grid, the quilt pattern may not be as clearly visible as you had hoped.

Another reason is that when you match up the seams with this trick, you can smooth out small discrepancies in patch size. While still piecing the block, you can ease in any excess and make less than perfect units fit. It is better to do it at the block level than trying to compensate for extra inches when sewing rows together. Of course if your 1/4-inch (6-mm) seam isn't the right size, it's best to adjust it as soon as you find out, but I'm not one to say you should throw away less than perfect blocks. If you are off by 1/8 inch (3 mm), you can definitely still make it work.

Notice how these corners do not perfectly match up as the seams have not been butted up.

4 Press the seam allowances in opposite directions (Row 1 to the left, Row 2 to the right, Row 3 to the left, etc). Pin butting seams (see page 57). Stitch to join the rows together.

Butting your seams will help you to make sure all your lines and joins are straight and precise.

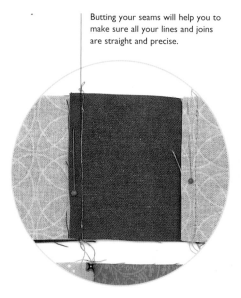

5 Continue until all the rows are joined.

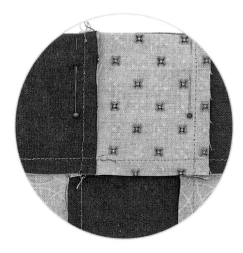

6 Press the long seams in one
direction and press again
from the front.

This patchwork block is called
"HALF-SQUARE TRIANGLES"

FABRICS

8 fabrics: 4 light and 4 dark

EQUIPMENT

- Acrylic ruler
- Pencil
- Rotary cutter
- Pins
- Iron

PATCHWORK

Piecing triangles from squares

Half-square triangles, or HSTs, are awesome!
So many amazing quilt patterns can come from
this humble little unit. Here they are arranged
with eight fabrics in groups of light and dark, but
rotate some of the units or try alternate color
placement and you've got a very different quilt
in front of you.

BLOCK DIAGRAM

Cut two 4-inch (10-cm)
squares from each fabric.

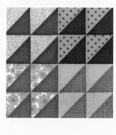

On the design wall

Using several of the same block together, with four blocks rotated so that the
triangles radiate out, can result in really different looks. Try it alternated with an
appliqué block, such as "Hawaiian Appliqué Block" (see pages 96–99).

I Using your acrylic ruler and only the four light fabrics, draw a diagonal line from corner to corner on the wrong side of each fabric square.

2 Pair up each light fabric with a dark fabric square, placing them right sides together. You should have four sets of squares, each with two fabrics. Pin down the center drawn line.

Hints and tips

SCARED OF SQUARES

Would you believe I was scared of HSTs for several years after I started quilting seriously? No matter what method I tried, I couldn't get them to come out square. The method covered in this technique teaches you to make them by first cutting generous squares, then stitching, slicing, pressing, and trimming them down to size. Once I realized I could fix any problems by trimming them down to size, the anxiety around HSTs started to melt away.

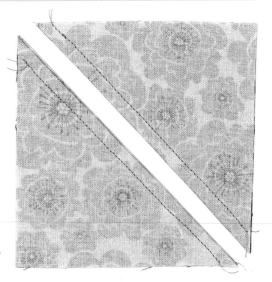

3 Take the first square to the sewing machine and sew ¼ inch (6 mm) away from the drawn line down one side. Lift your presser foot, gently pull out a bit of thread without cutting it, and rotate the block. Stitch ¼ inch (6 mm) away from the marked line on the other side. Repeat with the remaining sets. Press each square with a hot iron before cutting them apart—this will allow the stitches to "sink" into the fabric.

4 Using your acrylic ruler and rotary cutter, place the ruler on the drawn line and cut the patch corner to corner.

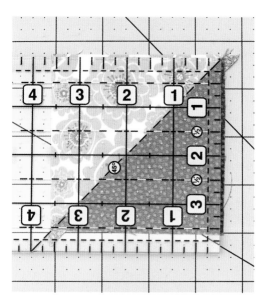

5 Open out each triangle unit and press, folding the dark fabric toward the seam allowance. This is called "pressing to the dark side." Repeat for all 16 patches.

6 Use the marked lines on your ruler and the 45-degree angle line to trim each block to 3½ inches (9 cm). You need the 45-degree line to match the center of your half-square triangle unit. Trim two sides, flip the block, and trim the remaining two.

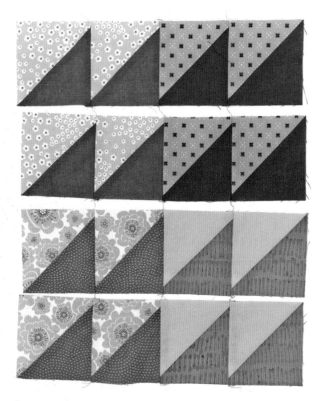

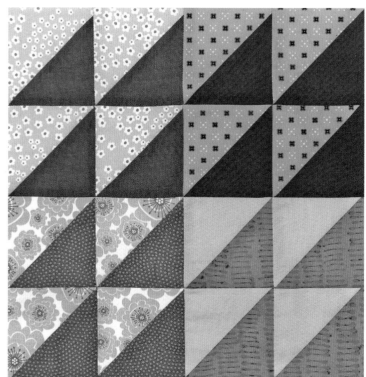

7 Arrange the 16 half-square triangle units as shown in the Block Diagram (see page 60). Stitch them together using the Chain Piecing method (see pages 56–59).

8 Press all the seams in one direction.

Nothing is quite as gratifying as a quick-to-piece but intricate-looking quilt of big, big, big half-square triangles. Starting with 10-inch (25.5-cm) squares in blues and yellow/orange, and using the methods taught on this page, I pieced this quilt top in a weekend.

PATCHWORK

Quarter-square triangles

Now that you've made some half-square triangles, let's try some quarter-square triangles, or QSTs. These units can be used in a variety of blocks to make stars, flowers, or butterflies, as shown in this example.

This patchwork block is called
"BUTTERFLIES"

FABRICS

2 colored fabrics and 1 neutral/light fabric

EQUIPMENT

* Acrylic ruler
* Pencil
* Rotary cutter
* Pins
* Iron

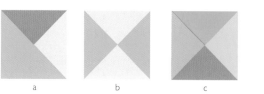

| a | b | c |

VARIATIONS

Combine a half-square triangle with a solid color to get the quarter-square unit that is used in this example (a). Combine two half-square triangles to get unit (b), sometimes called an hourglass. You could use four different colors for variation (c). Play around with value and fabric placement, and see what blocks you can come up with.

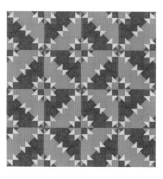

On the design wall

Play around by positioning several of the same block together. Rotate alternate blocks by 90 degrees and see a new pattern emerge (see left).

BLOCK DIAGRAM

* Cut two 4½-inch (11.5-cm) squares, three 3½-inch (9-cm) squares, and five 2½-inch (6.5-cm) squares from each colored fabric.
* Cut five 3-inch (7.5-cm) squares from the neutral fabric.

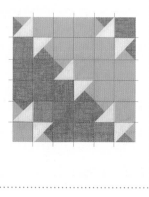

1 With your acrylic ruler and pencil, draw a diagonal line from corner to corner on the wrong side of the fabric of each of the five neutral fabric squares. Repeat with the 3½-inch (9-cm) squares of one of the other fabrics.

2 Pair up the two colored 3½-inch (9-cm) squares with the marked squares on top and right sides together. Pin down the center drawn line.

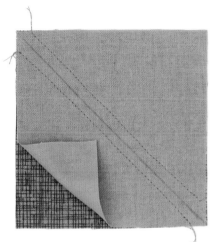

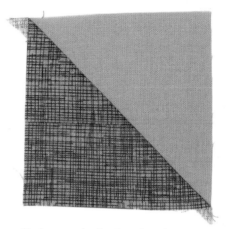

3 Stitch ¼ inch (6 mm) away from each side of the drawn line. Repeat for all three pairs.

4 Press each square with a hot iron, then cut the patches apart along the drawn line.

5 Open each triangle unit and press. Trim down to 3 inches (7.5 cm), making sure to match the center seam with the 45-degree line on your acrylic ruler. We only need five units for this block so just set one unit aside.

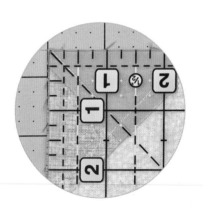

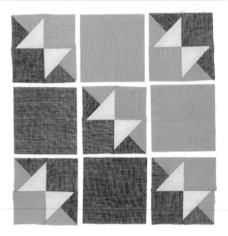

6 Pair each of the half-square triangles with a neutral square, making sure the drawn line on the square is perpendicular to the seam in the half-square triangle. Pin and stitch ¼ inch (6 mm) away from each side of the drawn line.

7 Press, cut apart, open, and press again, this time to the neutral fabric. (Although your seam allowance will be visible in the neutral-colored patches, this lessens bulk and will help your block lay flatter.) Use the marked lines on your ruler and the 45-degree angle line to trim each block to 2½ inches (6.5 cm). You will want the 45-degree line to match the center of your half-square triangle unit. Trim two corners, flip the block, and trim the remaining two.

8 Arrange the units as shown in the block diagram. First stitch the quarter-square triangles to the 2½-inch (6.5-cm) solid colored squares, making five four-patch units, or "butterfly" units (as shown in the four corners and center above). Press, then assemble the rest of the block using the Chain Piecing method shown on pages 56–69.

9 Press the long seams towards the center to reduce bulk.

This patchwork block is called
**"ECONOMY BLOCK
VARIATION"**

FABRICS

4 fabrics ranging from
light to dark.

EQUIPMENT

- Acrylic ruler
- Rotary cutter
- Pins
- Iron

Piecing bias-edged triangles

Triangles can strike fear into the hearts of even the most seasoned quilters. Why? Because bias-cut fabric stretches. On pages 60–63 we learned how to sew half-square triangles without sewing bias seams. Here we will take the plunge and cut the patches with bias edges. If you follow this pinch trick, use pins, and sew slowly, you'll lose that fear in no time. Remember, be gentle with your fabrics and they'll fit together beautifully.

BLOCK DIAGRAM

- Cut four 2½-inch (6.5-cm) squares from fabric A
- Cut five 2½-inch (6.5-cm) squares from fabric B.
- Cut one 7½-inch (19-cm) square from fabric C, then cut on the diagonal twice to make four triangles.
- Cut two 7-inch (18-cm) squares from fabric D, then cut each on the diagonal to make four triangles.

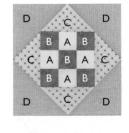

On the design wall

Use several of the same block together (see below) or alternate with "Granny Square" (see pages 68–69) or "Up and Out" (see below right and pages 70–73). This block has a strong outer edge so it plays well with other blocks both in alternating patterns and in rows.

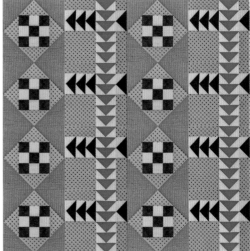

Use a fabric with a strong contrast for the corners of the 9-patch.

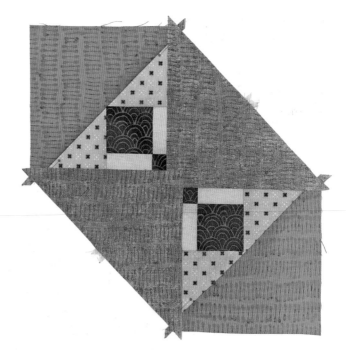

1 Take the four squares of fabric A and the five squares of fabric B and arrange in an alternating pattern to make a 9-patch unit. Stitch together, following the Chain Piecing method (see pages 56–59). Trim the unit down to a 6½-inch (16.5-cm) square.

2 Take one of the triangles in fabric C, fold it in half, and finger press or "pinch" the center to make a crease. Now fold the 9-patch unit in half horizontally and pinch along the crease.

3 Unfold both pieces and line up the creases—they should lie together smoothly. Carefully pin along the edge. Repeat with a second triangle in fabric C on the opposite side.

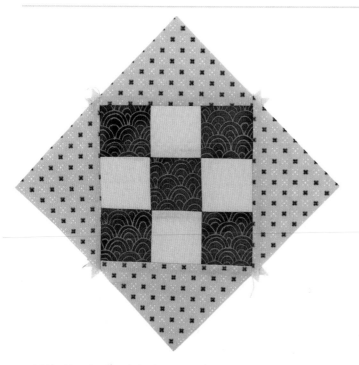

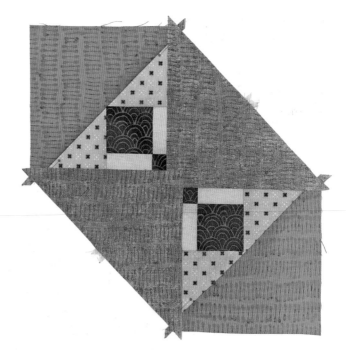

4 Working slowly, stitch along both edges, using a ¼-inch (6-mm) seam. Remove the pins and press with a hot iron, taking care not to distort the triangles while pressing. Repeat Steps 2 and 3 to fold, pinch, and stitch two more triangles to the remaining sides.

5 Repeat Steps 2–4 to add the four triangles in D. Press and then trim the block to a 12½-inch (31.5-cm) square.

This patchwork block is called
"GRANNY SQUARE"

Blocks on point

Triangles can also be used to shift the orientation of blocks so that they appear to be on the diagonal, or "On Point." In this technique, we learn how to cut squares into triangles and add them to the edges of the patchwork to support an on-point block. This technique can be used when setting finished blocks into a final quilt as well.

FABRICS

3 fabrics ranging from light to dark

EQUIPMENT

• Acrylic ruler
• Pencil
• Rotary cutter
• Pins
• Iron

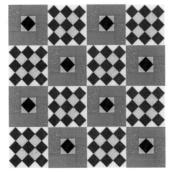

On the design wall

Try several of the same block together. This block works well as an alternate to non-diagonal blocks such as "Patio Bricks" (see left and pages 78–79) or could make a pretty impressive border to more subdued appliqué blocks teaming such as "Inside My Heart" (see pages 92–95).

BLOCK DIAGRAM

• Cut four 3⅜-inch (9.75-cm) squares from fabric A.
• Cut nine 3⅜-inch (9.75-cm) squares from fabric B.
• Cut two 5¼-inch (13.5-cm) squares from fabric C, then cut these on the diagonal twice to make eight setting triangles.
• Cut two 2⅞-inch (7.25-cm) squares from fabric C, then cut these on the diagonal to make four corner triangles.

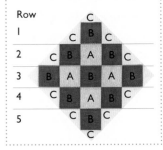

1 Arrange the squares as you'd like them. Start by sewing the A and B fabrics together with ¼-inch (6-mm) seams to make five strips, or diagonal rows as on the Block Diagram (see above).

Row 3

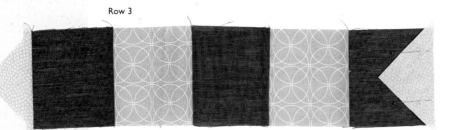

2 Attach a corner triangle to each end of Row 3. Use the pinch method (see Step 2, page 67) to align the triangles on either end of your row.

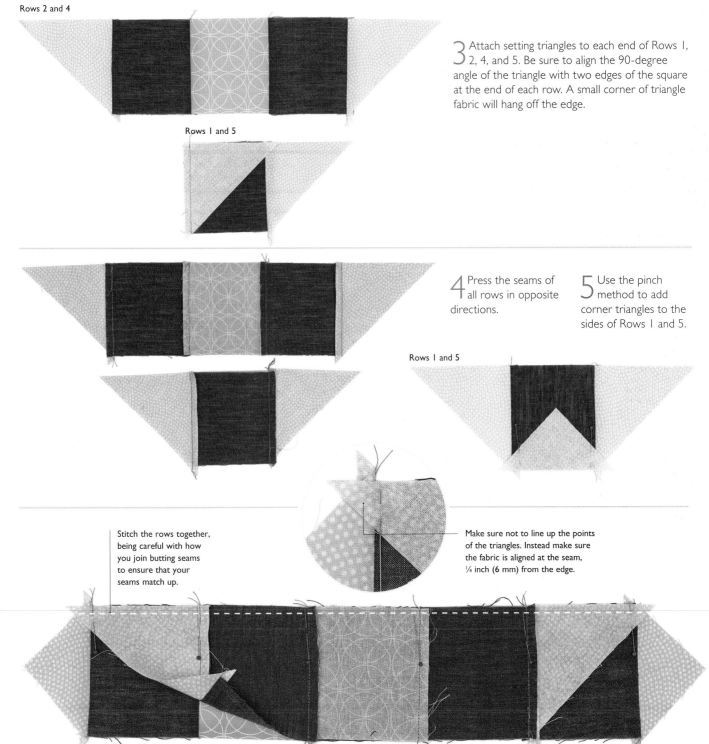

Rows 2 and 4

Rows 1 and 5

3 Attach setting triangles to each end of Rows 1, 2, 4, and 5. Be sure to align the 90-degree angle of the triangle with two edges of the square at the end of each row. A small corner of triangle fabric will hang off the edge.

4 Press the seams of all rows in opposite directions.

5 Use the pinch method to add corner triangles to the sides of Rows 1 and 5.

Rows 1 and 5

Stitch the rows together, being careful with how you join butting seams to ensure that your seams match up.

Make sure not to line up the points of the triangles. Instead make sure the fabric is aligned at the seam, ¼ inch (6 mm) from the edge.

Row 3 with Row 2 on top

6 Pin butting seams. Start pinning from the center and work out toward the triangles. Be careful not to stretch the triangle points. Join Rows 1–5.

7 Press all the seams in one direction. Square up the block to get rid of the triangle tags along the edges.

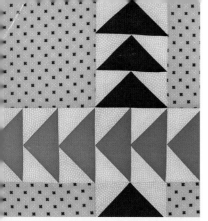

This patchwork block is called
"UP AND OUT"

FABRICS

4 fabrics: 1 for the block background, 1 for the background to the "geese"—the "sky"—and 2 for the "geese."

EQUIPMENT

• Pins
• Pencil
• Acrylic ruler
• Rotary cutter
• Iron

No-waste flying geese

"Flying Geese" are a really awesome block unit because they are very versatile and add so much movement to your quilt. The no-waste method we will learn while creating this block allows you to get two "geese" without cutting any triangles or sewing any bias edges.

On the design wall

Use several of the same block together but make the geese with a variety of fabrics (below left). Scrappy chaos can really be harnessed into a powerful quilt with this block. It also alternates well with "Economy Block Variation" (see pages 66–67) or "Starry Night" (see below right and pages 106–109).

BLOCK DIAGRAM

• From the background fabric, cut: one 6½-inch (16.5-cm) square, one 2½-inch (6.5-cm) square, and two rectangles, each measuring 6½ × 2½ inches (16.5 × 6.5 cm).
• Cut two 5¼-inch (13.5-cm) squares from "Goose A."
• Cut three 5¼-inch (13.5-cm) squares from "Goose B."
• Cut 20 2⅞-inch (7.2-cm) squares from the "sky" fabric. The "geese" finish at 2 × 4 inches (5 × 10 cm).

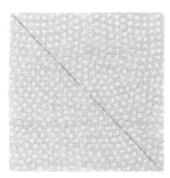

1 Start by taking all of the "sky" squares which will form the background to the "geese" and drawing a diagonal line down the back from corner to corner.

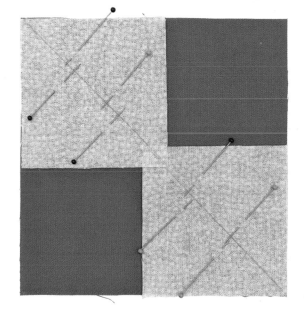

2 Layer two "sky" squares in opposite corners on one larger "goose" square, aligning the drawn lines. Pin into place.

3 Stitch ¼ inch (6 mm) away from the drawn line on both sides. Press with a hot iron before cutting apart on the drawn line.

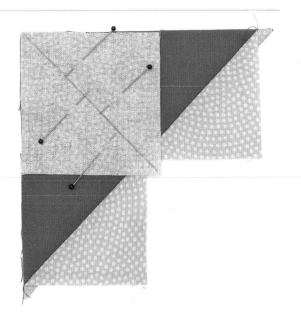

4 Press the seam allowance toward the "sky" triangles and pin another sky square to each unit.

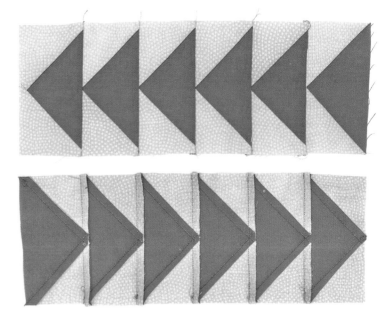

5 Stitch ¼ inch (6 mm) away from the drawn line on both sides. Press with a hot iron before cutting apart on the line. Press the seam allowance toward the "sky" triangle and trim the unit to 2½ × 4½ inches (6.5 × 11.5 cm).

6 Repeat Steps 2–5 for all goose units. One large square and four small squares makes a total of four geese units. Join six geese units in a row and press seam allowances in the direction the geese are "flying."

7 Assemble the block units as shown in the Block Diagram on page 70, first sewing two background pieces to the upward-pointing geese unit, then two background pieces to the lone lower goose. Finally, attach the three segments.

8 Give the block a good press and you're done!

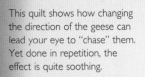

This quilt shows how changing
the direction of the geese can
lead your eye to "chase" them.
Yet done in repetition, the
effect is quite soothing.

This patchwork block is called
"54–40 OR FIGHT"

FABRICS

3 fabrics (red, white, and blue)

EQUIPMENT

- Pins
- Acrylic templates (Tri-Recs), or use the templates on page 152
- Rotary cutter
- Iron

Using acrylic templates

Not every quilt block is easily cut with your acrylic ruler and rotary cutter. Some angles are better achieved with specialty templates, like this "54–40 or Fight" block that uses 60-degree triangles. The acrylic templates have special markings or cutouts, which make it easy to cut patches from strips and align the patches when stitching the block by machine. Manufacturers produce a lot of specialty templates to make cutting easier for today's quilter. Ask if your local fabric store carries any, or search online with the block name and "acrylic templates" (see Resources, page 154).

On the design wall

This block makes a bold statement when alternated with others. When paired with curved appliqué (such as "Ainu-Inspired Freehand Spiral," see below left and pages 110–111) or triangles piecing (such as "Economy Block Variation," see below right and pages 66–67), the four-patch units in the corners of this block create a secondary pattern of diagonal lines across the quilt top.

BLOCK DIAGRAM

- From the red fabric, cut: one rectangle, 2½ × 6 inches (6.5 × 15 cm) and one strip, 4½ × 14 inches (11.5 × 35.5 cm).
- From the white fabric, cut: one rectangle, 2½ × 6 inches (6.5 × 15 cm), one strip, 4½ × 13 inches (11.5 × 33 cm), and one strip, 2½ × 22 inches (6.5 × 56 cm).
- Cut one strip, 2½ × 22 inches (6.5 × 56 cm) from the blue fabric.

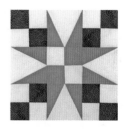

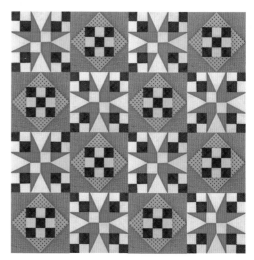

CUTTING WITH TRI-RECS RULERS

Most specialty templates come with their own cutting instructions, as well as guide marks for cutting a variety of sizes of block units. Here we need 4-inch (10-cm) finished units for our block. The Tri-Recs instructions say to cut strips that are 4½ inches (11.5 cm) wide. If you do not have the Tri-Recs tool, use the template on page 152 to cut your patches. When paired, a Tri unit and two Recs units will always make a triangle within a square.

Cutting

To cut Tri triangles, first cut the appropriate strip width (in this instance 4½ inches/11.5 cm). Lay the top edge of the tool along the top edge of the strip and align the bottom of the strip with the appropriate line on the tool. Cut on both sides of the tool.

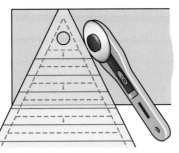

Rotate the tool, align the top edge of the tool with the bottom of the strip and the top of the strip with the appropriate line on the tool. Cut as indicated.

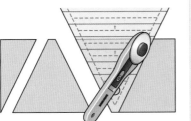

To cut Recs triangles, cut the same size strip as you did for the Tri triangles. Fold the strip right sides together to automatically cut both a right and a left triangle. Align the top of the tool with the top of the strip as shown. Cut on both sides of the tool. Trim off the "magic angle." This will make alignment for piecing a breeze.

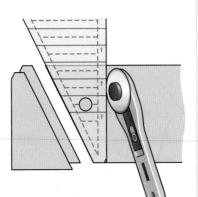

Rotate the tool, align the top edge of the tool with the bottom of the strip and the top of the strip with the appropriate line on the tool. Cut.

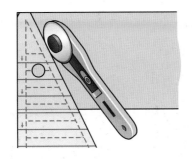

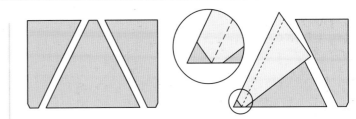

Piecing triangles within squares

With right sides together, lay one Recs triangle on the left side of the Tri triangle as shown. Note the alignment of the "magic angle" on the Recs triangle with the bottom of the Tri triangle. Align the long edges as shown and stitch. Press. With right sides together, stitch the second Recs triangle to the right side of the Tri triangle to complete the square. Press seams toward the Recs triangles. Trim the "dog-ears" and include in your pieced block.

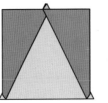
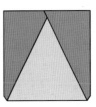

| Triangle within a square | Dog-ears trimmed | With ¼ inch (6 mm) seams removed |

Piecing rectangles

Place two Recs triangles right sides together, aligning the "magic angle" as shown. Stitch and press toward the darker fabric. Trim the "dog-ears" and include in your pieced block.

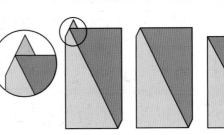

With ¼ inch (6 mm) seams removed

1 Start by sewing strip sets of red and white and blue and white (see pages 52–53), then sub-cut the sets into 2½-inch (6.5-cm) widths. You will have two red and white units and eight blue and white units.

 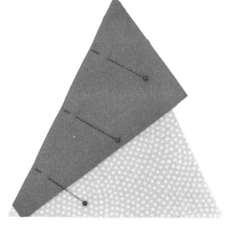 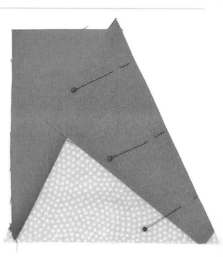

2 Press and flip the 2½-inch (6.5-cm) squares and piece them into 4-patch units, each measuring 4½ inches (11.5 cm). You will have one red and white unit and four blue and white units.

3 Make the star points by sewing a red triangle to one side of a white triangle.

4 Open and press before pinning the next red triangle to the white triangle. Repeat for a total of four star point units.

5 Arrange the units as shown in the Block Diagram (see page 74). Stitch them together, using the Chain Piecing method (see pages 56–59).

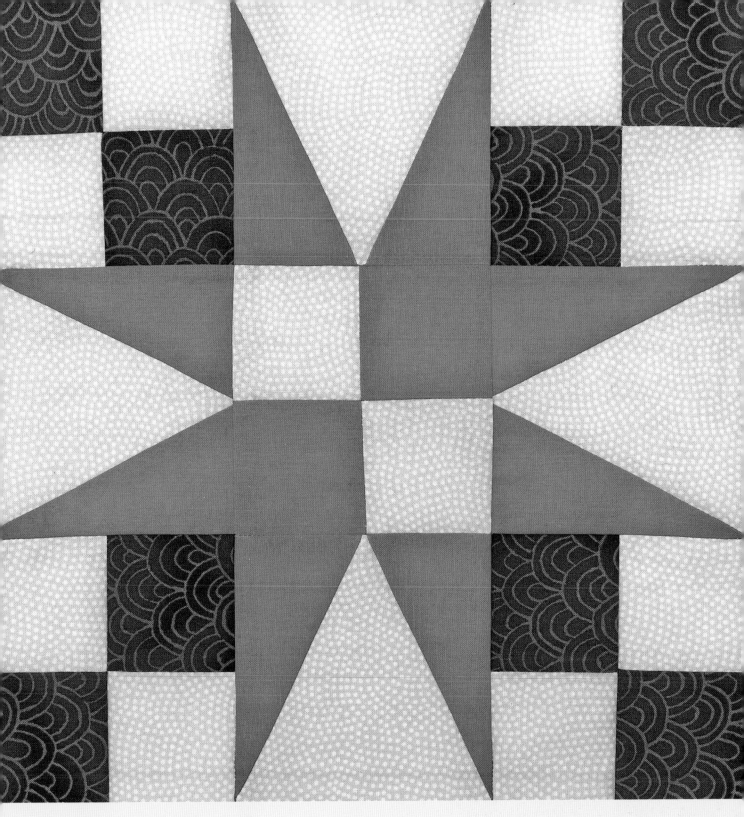

6 Press all the seams in one
direction, and the block is
now complete.

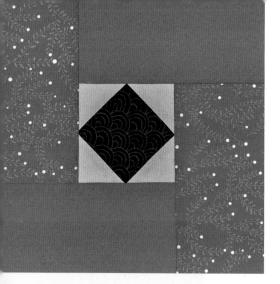

This patchwork block is called
"PATIO BRICKS"

FABRICS

3 fabrics (red, white, and blue)

EQUIPMENT
• Pins
• Rotary cutter
• Iron

Sewing partial seams

Not all quilt blocks fit on a traditional 3 × 3, 5 × 5, or 6 × 6 grid. In this technique, we will practice sewing a partial seam by adding slabs around a central patch. This block pieces quickly but the intermediate skill adds a level of sophistication to your quilt project.

BLOCK DIAGRAM
• Cut four 4½- × 8½-inch (11.5- × 21.5-cm) rectangles from the red fabric (two varying red fabrics can be used, as here).
• Cut two 2⅞-inch (7.25-cm) squares from the white fabric, then cut each once on the diagonal to make four triangles.
• Cut one 3⅜-inch (9-cm) square from the blue fabric.

On the design wall

Use several of the same block together for a pleasing, symmetrical pattern. Alternating this block with any appliqué block will create an interesting design, such as with the "Inside My Heart" block (see left and pages 92–95).

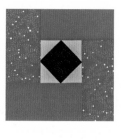

1 Start by sewing a square in a square unit like the center of an Economy Block (see Steps 2–4, page 67).

2 Lay the square unit face down on your first red rectangle, aligning the bottom edge. Pin along the right side. Start sewing approximately 1 inch (2.5 cm) down from the top of the square patch.

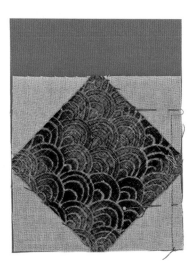

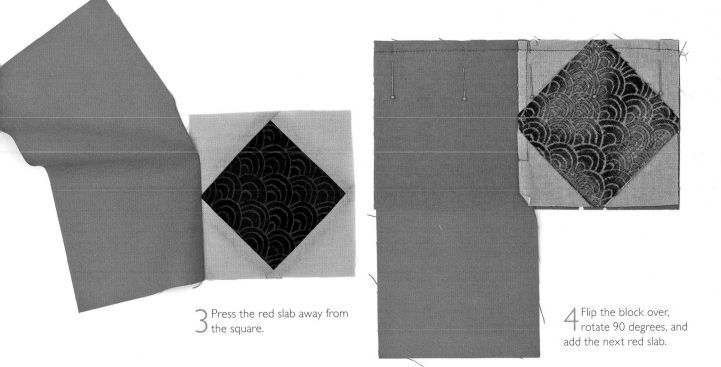

3 Press the red slab away from the square.

4 Flip the block over, rotate 90 degrees, and add the next red slab.

5 Press each slab away from the center and continue rotating the piece and adding red slabs.

6 Once the fourth slab has been sewn in place, press it open, and then fold the block to align the last seam. Pin and sew from the slab edge to the stitches in the central square. Press seams and the block is finished.

This patchwork block is called
"DRUNKARD'S PATH"

FABRICS

4 fabrics in contrasting pairs,
or scraps with high contrast.

EQUIPMENT

- Pins
- Pencil
- Acrylic ruler
- Rotary cutter
- Iron
- Templates (see page 152)

PATCHWORK

Curved piecing

Are you ready to try some curves? They are not as hard as they look, and once you get a feel for them, you'll be ready to try out a bunch of other traditional curved block patterns that you come across. The trick is to pin, pin, pin, and to sew slow. The quarter circle, or "Drunkard's Path," block is an excellent beginners' curve because it is symmetrical and versatile. In this section, we will make 16 quarter circles. Arrange them as shown or play around to see what other layouts appeal to you.

BLOCK DIAGRAM

Cut four 3½-inch (9-cm) squares and four 2½-inch (6.5-cm) squares from each fabric.

On the design wall

Use several of the same block together in varying color combinations (below left). Use this block in a design with "Dresden Plate" (see below right and pages 88–91) for an interesting central motif.

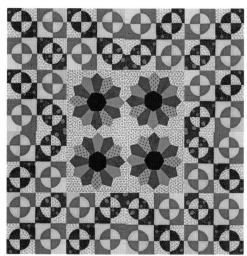

1 Photocopy the templates on page 152 onto lightweight paper and cut out. Place the quarter-circle template onto a small fabric square and the corner template onto a larger fabric square in the contrasting color, aligning the edges. Pin and mark the curved line. Remove the templates and carefully cut along the marked lines.

2 Mark the centers of each patch by folding and pinching or ironing to make a crease. Fold the outer patches with right sides together, and the inner patches with wrong sides together.

3 Align the creases and pin with the outer patch on top. Start in the center, pin the left edge, and work the fabric in your fingers to align the seam-allowance edges between the center and edge pins. Place one or two pins between the others. Repeat for the right edge and center.

4 Start sewing by putting the left edge under the presser foot and carefully pulling the fabric flat as you guide it under the needle. Go slow and stop to readjust the fabric the first few times.

5 Press the unit with the seam allowance toward the center (smaller patch).

6 Repeat to make three more units in this color set. Assemble them into a four-patch block.

7 Repeat with the other fabric sets, join them into four-patch circle units and stitch those up into a finished block.

This patchwork block is called
"LIGHT AND SHADOW"

FABRICS

4 different colored fabrics

EQUIPMENT

• Templates (see page 153)
• Pins
• Acrylic ruler
• Rotary cutter
• Iron

Foundation paper piecing

Add dramatic angles to your blocks with striking accuracy—welcome to the world of foundation paper piecing. This technique is all about straight lines and matching points. The "Light and Shadow" block demonstrated here is a great beginner tool to get your feet wet with foundation paper piecing. It's tough to get your brain to "sew backward" at first, but once you get the hang of it, the units will fly from your machine with amazing precision.

BLOCK DIAGRAM

Cut a 9 × 11 inch (23 × 28 cm) rectangle of each of your four fabrics.

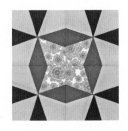

On the design wall

Using several of the same block together creates an almost hypnotic effect (below left). This block also looks striking combined with "English Paper Pieced Hexagon Star (see below right and pages 102–105).

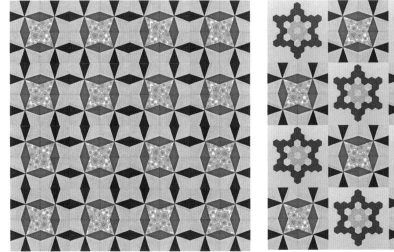

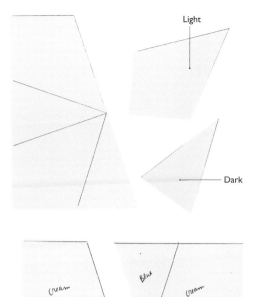

Light

Dark

1 Photocopy five copies of the template on page 153 onto lightweight paper. Carefully cut out each on the thick black line. On one copy, cut out the two template shapes—light and dark.

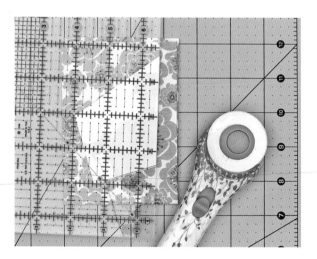

2 On the remaining four templates, write your fabric colors where you want them to end up (this will help avoid confusion in a minute).

Fix-it
ADJUST YOUR STITCH LENGTH

When using paper as a foundation, it is important to reduce the stitch length on your machine to make it easier to remove the papers in the end. A stitch length of 2.2 is fine for sewing fabric to fabric, but lower the stitch length to 1.8–1.6 when stitching fabric to paper. A shorter stitch length will basically perforate the paper, making it easier to tear on the dotted line when you are ready to remove it. Like any perforated paper (think coupons, etc), it helps to fold along the line you plan to tear before just ripping it off.

Watch out! Always make sure that you have enough thread in your bobbin before starting a foundation paper pieced block—if the needle perforates the paper but nothing is sewn, that line will become very weak if/ when you need to stitch over it again. You don't want your foundation to tear away too soon.

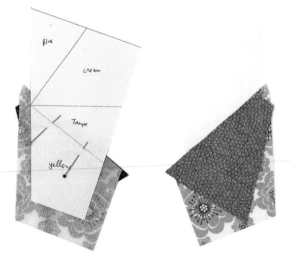

3 Take the two paper templates (one kite shape and one triangle), and use them to cut out your fabrics using the templates you labeled in Step 2 to guide you on the numbers and shapes you need in each fabric. Fold the fabric so you can cut 2–4 units at a time, then lay the paper template on top and cut around it with a ½-inch (1.3-cm) seam allowance.

4 Take one foundation paper and place two fabric pieces face to face. Align them on the wrong side of the paper with a seam allowance of over ¼ inch (6 mm) crossing over the line. Hold it up to the light to see how it looks. Place one pin to hold them to the paper.

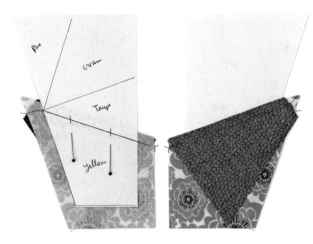

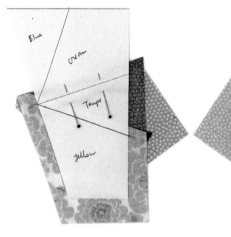

5 Lower your stitch length and sew the two fabrics onto the paper by stitching on the marked line.

6 Open the fabrics and press with a dry iron. Trim the second fabric to a ¼-inch (6-mm) seam allowance if necessary. Align the next fabric and pin into place.

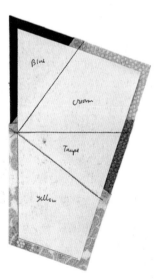

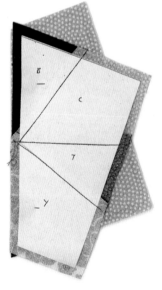

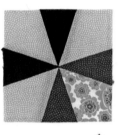

9 Remove the foundation paper pieces carefully. The edges of the block are all cut on the bias, so be careful not to distort them.

7 Stitch and press until all the fabrics are sewn onto the foundation. Trim the excess fabric so that there is only ¼ inch (6 mm) around the foundation paper.

8 Repeat this sequence seven times. Join two units to make a 6½-inch (16.5-cm) unfinished square. Carefully align the foundation papers when joining the halves of one unit. Press that seam open to avoid bulk at the center.

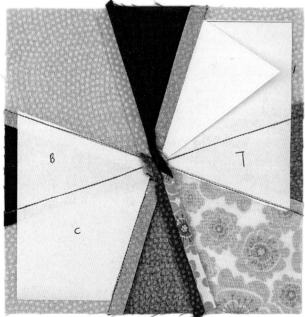

10 Join four squares together to make the final block,
referring to the Block Diagram on page 84.

This appliqué block is called
"DRESDEN PLATE"

FABRICS

At least 5 fabrics: 1 for the background, 1 for the central hexagon, and 3 or more for the petals

EQUIPMENT

• Templates (see page 155)
• Pins
• Acrylic ruler
• Rotary cutter
• Iron
• Hand-appliqué tools: thimble, needle, thread

APPLIQUÉ

Whipstitching for appliqué

Let's start our foray into appliqué with a machine-pieced and hand-appliquéd "Dresden Plate" block. Stitch the petals together by machine, pin the plate into place, and practice your whipstitch to secure it to the background fabric. Cover the hole in the center with a big hexagon and stand back to admire this simple yet impressive block.

BLOCK DIAGRAM

• Cut one 13-inch (33-cm) square from the background fabric.
• Cut 12 petals from three or more petal fabrics using the template on page 152.
• Cut one 4½-inch (11.5-cm) square from the central hexagon fabric.

On the design wall

Use several of the same block together to create a bold-looking design (below left). Alternate with "Butterflies" made with the same fabrics as the petals and let the colors play off each other (see below right and pages 64–65).

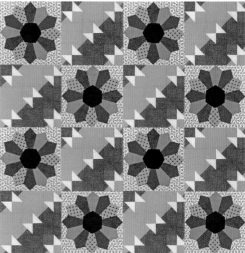

1 Fold one petal in half lengthwise, with right sides together, and stitch a ¼-inch (6-mm) seam along the top (wider) edge. Repeat this for all 12 petals.

2 Turn each petal right side out and press with a hot iron. The seam should be pressed to one side.

3 Join the petals in a ring, pressing seams open. Stitch the first six together, then the next six, then pin and join the two halves. This is a Dresden ring.

Press seams open so the appliqué will lie flat against the background.

4 Fold the square of background fabric in quarters and press the folds to make creases. Open and align the ring evenly in the center of the square.

5 Thread-baste the Dresden ring onto the background fabric. Begin appliquéing by securing a knotted thread in one petal's seam allowance and taking small whipstitches along the edge of the ring. Appliqué along the entire outer edge of the ring.

6 Baste the central hexagon fabric onto the hexagon template on page 152 (see pages 44–45 for instructions on how to do this). Carefully remove the template with your finger and press the hexagon with a hot iron.

7 Align the hexagon over the hole in the ring and pin into place. Secure a knotted thread, as in Step 5, and appliqué the hexagon to the ring, carefully catching the background fabric as you stitch.

8 Remove all pins and basting thread and give the block a gentle press. Trim to a 12½-inch (31.5-cm) square and you're done.

This appliqué block is called
"INSIDE MY HEART"

FABRICS

2 fabrics: 1 background fabric
(this fabric goes on top) and
1 focus fabric (this fabric goes
underneath)

EQUIPMENT

• Appliqué design to transfer
  (see pages 154–155)
• Masking tape
• Pencil
• Pins
• Fabric scissors
• Basting thread
• Iron
• Hand-appliqué tools: thimble,
  needle, thread

Reverse needleturn appliqué

Reverse needleturn appliqué is where a
design is cut into one fabric that is then
placed over another, and when the
design is stitched, the bottom fabric
shows through. In this block, we will
stitch three hearts inside one another
and then snip away the excess bottom
fabric to reduce the bulk. See how
easily a simple line drawing can add
impact to your quilt.

BLOCK DIAGRAM

Cut one 13-inch (33-cm)
square from each of your
fabrics.

On the design wall

Use several of the same block together and rotate them for a playful layout
(below left). Alternate with a patchwork block like "Trip Around The World"
(see below right and pages 56–59) to give the smooth lines of the appliqué
more structure.

USING A LIGHTBOX TO TRANSFER A PATTERN

To recreate this block, you will need to transfer the design from paper onto your fabric before you can cut and sew. Start by copying the design on pages 154–155 onto paper (either trace it or use a photocopier). Next, use a lightbox or a sunny window to help transfer the design. Tape the design to the light box or window, then tape the fabric on top. Turn the light on (or use the sunlight) so you can see the design through your fabric. Hold the fabric steady and gently trace the design onto your fabric with a pencil. Remove the tape and you're ready to layer your appliqué block. On a light-colored fabric, use a thin pencil line or water-soluble fabric marker so that the marked lines do not show through after the piece is stitched.

1 Take the top (background) fabric and fold it into quarters. Crease the centerfold with a hot iron (see Hand-Appliqué Basics, pages 42–43). Open the fabric and trace the design using the pattern on pages 154–155 and a lightbox or sunny window (see panel above). Make sure to align the crease with the small cross in the center of the pattern before you begin.

2 Lay the top fabric on top of the bottom (focus) fabric and pin in a few places. Use basting thread to baste about ¾ inch (2 cm) away from all marked lines. One line of basting between the marked lines is enough.

3 Using pointed fabric scissors, carefully cut along the traced line of the center heart through the top fabric only. Be careful not to cut into the bottom fabric. Cut each heart design after the previous one is sewn, this will help the top fabric retain strength as you handle it.

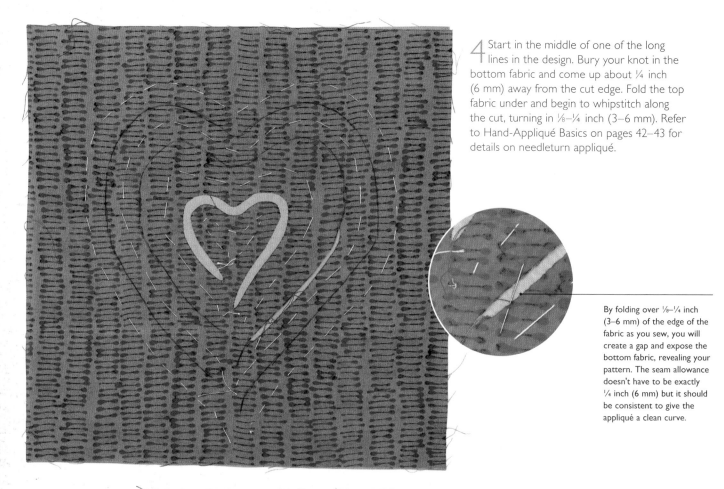

4 Start in the middle of one of the long lines in the design. Bury your knot in the bottom fabric and come up about ¼ inch (6 mm) away from the cut edge. Fold the top fabric under and begin to whipstitch along the cut, turning in ⅛–¼ inch (3–6 mm). Refer to Hand-Appliqué Basics on pages 42–43 for details on needleturn appliqué.

By folding over ⅛–¼ inch (3–6 mm) of the edge of the fabric as you sew, you will create a gap and expose the bottom fabric, revealing your pattern. The seam allowance doesn't have to be exactly ¼ inch (6 mm) but it should be consistent to give the appliqué a clean curve.

5 Continue turning under using the needle to guide the fabric as you appliqué along both sides of the marked line. Once all raw edges are sewn, remove the basting thread and give the block a gentle press. Flip the block over and trim away the excess fabric, leaving ½–1 inch (1.3–2.5 cm) around the edge of the outermost stitches.

At the end of a length of thread, bury the thread tails behind the top of the fabric so that the stitches don't show through to the front of the block.

6 Trim the block to 12½ inches (31.5 cm)
square and you're done.

Hawaiian appliqué

This appliqué block is called **"HAWAIIAN APPLIQUÉ BLOCK"**

FABRICS

2 fabrics: 1 background fabric and 1 focus fabric

EQUIPMENT

- Templates (see page 153)
- Pins
- Fabric scissors
- Basting thread
- Iron
- Hand-appliqué tools: thimble, needle, thread

Hawaiian appliqué is a beautiful tradition. It is a bit like cutting out a paper snowflake—fabric is folded into eighths and a continuous line shape is cut through all layers, then opened onto a background fabric and appliquéd in place with a continuous whipstitch. Try this simple flower block to learn the skills of needleturn appliqué, points, and valleys. Make sure to check out the back side of the block from time to time: your stitches will improve before you're half way around, it's quite amazing!

BLOCK DIAGRAM

- Cut one 13-inch (33-cm) square from the background fabric.
- Cut one 12-inch (30.5-cm) square from the focus fabric.

On the design wall

Use this block multiple times to create a dramatic all-over pattern (see left). It would also work well combined with alternate "Patio Bricks" (see pages 78–79). If several blocks together looks too busy, try adding wide sashing in a similar or contrasting color to the background.

PERFECTLY POSITIONING YOUR MOTIF

Once you've removed the paper template (Step 4), align the folded edge of the flower with a crease on the square of background fabric, placing the point in the center. Carefully unfold one section at a time by sliding your hand under the fold and flipping it over. Always make sure the creases in the two fabrics are properly aligned before moving on to the next fold.

Start by folding your 13-inch (33-cm) square of background fabric into eights and pressing to crease it with a hot iron. Press each fold as you make it for nice sharp creases.

2 Take the 12-inch (30.5-cm) square of focus fabric and fold it in eights, right sides together, and press each fold with a hot iron to crease it. Align the paper template on the folded focus-fabric triangle—the center line should match up with the long fold in the fabric. Pin the template in place.

3 Using sharp fabric scissors, carefully cut out the flower about ¼ inch (6 mm) away from the paper template. When you get to the tight spaces and deep valleys between the petals and leaves, cut right in between the paper template, leaving seam allowances on either side of the cut. Do not cut along the long fold!

4 Remove the paper template and lay the folded flower on top of your background fabric. Carefully align the creases and open the flower appliqué, one fold at a time, spreading it onto the background fabric gently. See Perfectly Positioning Your Motif, left. Pin in several places.

5 Baste the flower to the background with basting thread, about ½–¾ inch (1.3–2 cm) away from the raw edge.

6 Begin needleturn appliqué, paying close attention to the points and valleys. See pages 42–43 for more information on the needleturn technique.

7 Once you have appliquéd the entire block, remove the basting thread and give the block a gentle press. Trim to a 12½-inch (31.5-cm) square and your block is done.

In this beautiful example of a Hawaiian sampler quilt, the colors of the appliqué fabric are alternated to add more interest.

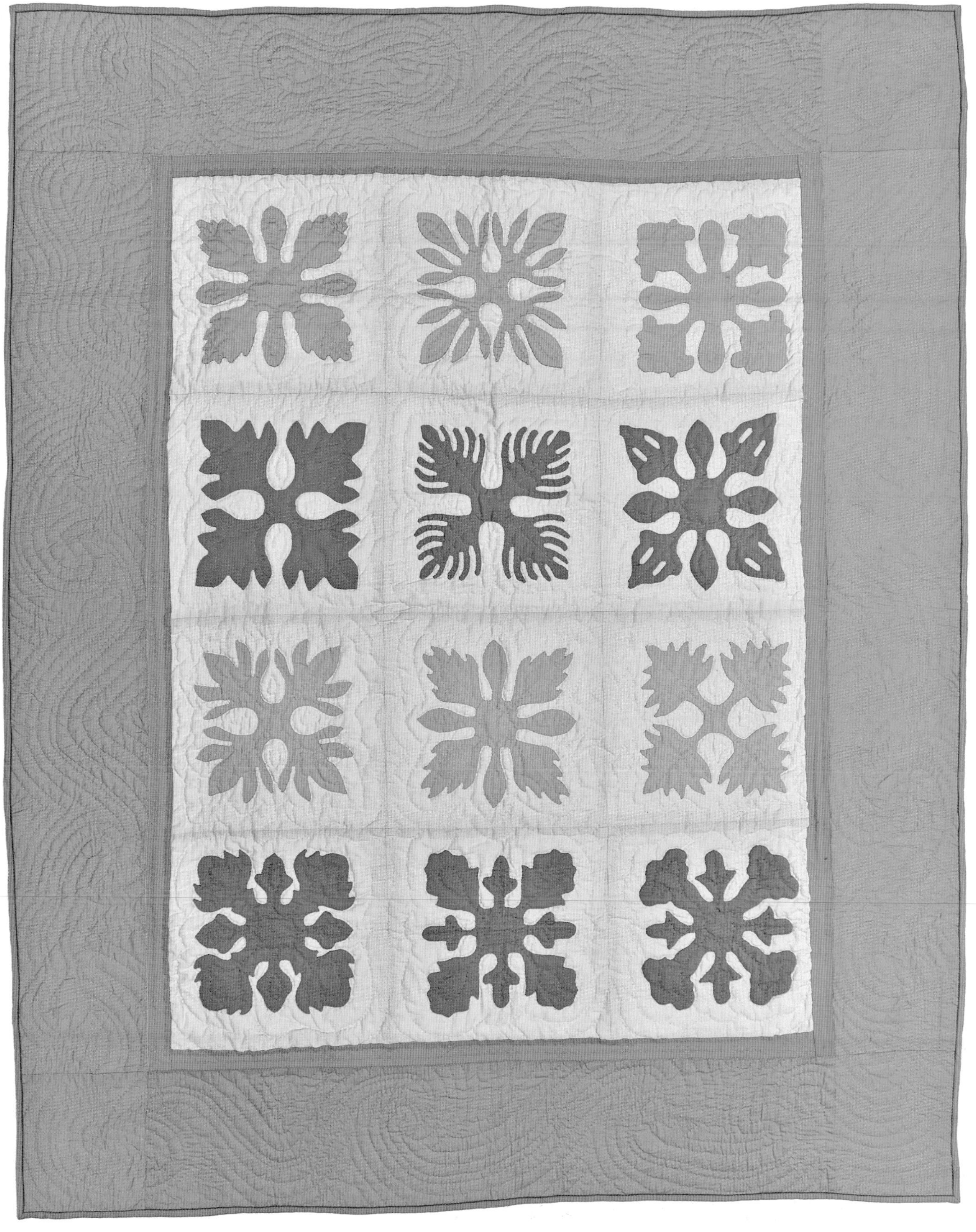

This appliqué block is called
"LARGE PRINT APPLIQUÉ"

FABRICS

2 fabrics: 1 dark fabric for
the background and 1 or
more printed fabrics for the
appliqué motifs

EQUIPMENT

- Pins
- Scissors
- Basting thread
- Acrylic ruler
- Rotary cutter
- Iron
- Hand-appliqué tools:
  thimble, needle, thread

APPLIQUÉ

Appliqué with patterned fabric

The technique of cutting out motifs from patterned fabric and appliquéing them to a blank background is quite old and often called *Broderie Perse*. Here, flowers from a busy print are cut out with a small ring in a dark background fabric surrounding them, and then appliquéd into a wreath on a square of the background fabric. Try using different types of printed fabric to make blocks with lots of personality.

BLOCK DIAGRAM

- Cut one 13-inch (33-cm) square from the background fabric.
- Cut 6–9 motifs from the patterned fabric. Make sure to cut a generous seam allowance on each piece so that part of the original background can be seen around the image after it is appliquéd.

On the design wall

Use several of the same block together for a beauiful, all-over design (below left). Try combining this block with "Starry Night" (see pages 106–109) or "Granny Square" (see below right and pages 68–69). Make your appliqué blocks stretch further by alternating or combining with machine-pieced patchwork.

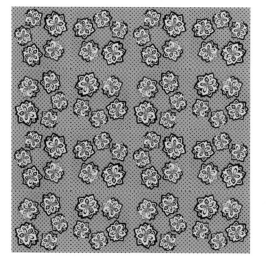

1 Select a medium- to large-print fabric with motifs that are separate enough to be cut out individually. This is your focus fabric. See the panel on page 27 for tips on how to choose the right fabrics for this technique.

2 Using fabric scissors, cut out 6–9 motifs from your focus print.

3 Fold the square of background fabric in quarters and press to crease. Open up the square and lay out the cutouts to form a wreath shape. Pin in place.

4 Using basting thread, baste about ½–¾ inches (1.3–2 cm) in from the raw edge on all the cutouts.

5 Using the needleturn method, appliqué the shapes in place. For a review of hand-appliqué basics, see pages 42–43.

6 Once all of the shapes are appliquéd in place, remove the basting thread, give the block a good press from the back side, and trim to 12½ inches (31.5cm) square.

APPLIQUÉ

Appliquéing English paper piecing

Many quilters love English paper piecing (EPP)
for its accuracy, portability, and limitless design
possibilities. Check out the Basics of English Paper
Piecing on pages 44–45 and become familiar with
that technique before moving on to this lesson.
Here, 37 English paper pieced hexagons are
joined to make a star, which will be appliquéd to
a background square.

BLOCK DIAGRAM

- Cut one 13½-inch (34.5-cm)
  square of the background
  fabric.
- For the hexagons, cut 2-inch
  (5-cm) squares as follows:
  6 squares from fabric A,
  7 squares from fabric B,
  24 squares from fabric C.

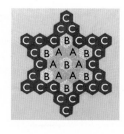

On the design wall

Combine with other star blocks like "Starry Night" (see below right and pages
106–109) for a thematic design. Repeat fabrics in several types of star blocks
for a unified thematic design. Try multiple repeats of the same design or team
with other scrappy blocks such as "Improv Strings" (see pages 120–123) to
show off lots of fabrics and textures.

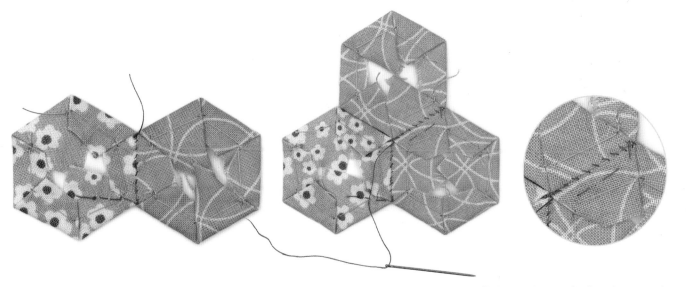

1 Cover each hexagon template in one of the 2-inch (5-cm) fabric squares (see pages 44–45). Start by sewing the six hexagons in fabric A around one hexagon in fabric B. Hold two templates right sides together, secure with a knot (see below), and whipstitch from corner to corner.

2 Open them up and add a third hexagon, making sure to align all six corners. Make a wrap knot in the corner and whipstitch another seam.

3 Backtrack to get back to the center by taking a few stitches in the seam allowance to bring your needle to the corner you wish to sew from. Add the next hexagon and continue.

SECURE THOSE KNOTS!

When joining hexagons or other EPP shapes, make a habit of burying your knot in the seam allowance on the back of your piece. Start by making a knot in the thread, then take three stitches through the seam allowance, bringing your needle up at the corner where you want to start. Whipstitch the patches together and when you're at the end of your thread, take a few backstitches over the stitches you've just sewn, then bury the thread in the seam allowance again. These extra steps will make the back of your piece nice and tidy (no stray threads flying loose) and your knots secure—when the kids or your dog jump on the quilt, your knots won't pop through to the front!

4 Once the first rosette is finished, join the next ring, alternating fabrics B and C as shown.

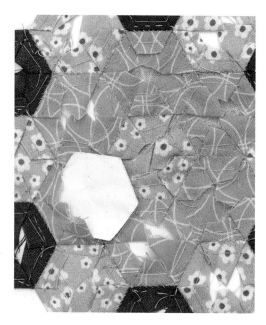

5 Remove the paper templates once all the seams have been sewn (see page 45).

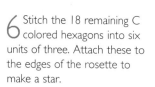

6 Stitch the 18 remaining C colored hexagons into six units of three. Attach these to the edges of the rosette to make a star.

Use a contrasting colored basting thread so that it is easy to see to remove.

7 Remove all the paper templates and give the star a good press. Mark the center of the background square by folding in half and pressing to make a crease. Position the Hexagon Star in the center of the fabric and thread-baste into place.

8 Appliqué the star to the background fabric using whipstitch (see pages 42–43) and then give it a good press from the back. Trim the block to a 12½-inch (31.5-cm) square, making sure you center the star before cutting.

Instead of appliquéing individual stars to background fabric, hexagon units can be used to piece the stars together in a variety of designs. Here, colored scraps form stars separated by a mix of neutral fabrics in a Seven Sisters pattern.

This improv block is called
"STARRY NIGHT"

FABRICS

At least 3 fabrics: 1 for the
background (at least a fat quarter)
and 2 or more for the stars

EQUIPMENT

- Pins
- Acrylic ruler
- Rotary cutter
- Iron

IMPROV

Improvisational stars

Stars are a very prevalent motif in quilting and
it's fun to play with this shape without worrying
about rules. In this technique we will learn to
add triangles to squares to make star points, then
combine two small star units into a larger block.
Don't let the small size of the patches put you
off, this is the perfect way to use up those fabric
scraps that are too tiny for other blocks but too
precious or beautiful to throw away.

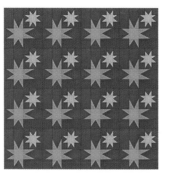

On the design wall

Try creating several of the same
block and piecing them together,
combining with plain colored blocks,
or with other patterned blocks such
as "Butterflies" (see pages 64–65).
This block can also be rotated to
create more options. Four "Starry
Night" blocks, each rotated 90
degrees, will make a ring of stars
appear (see page 109).

BLOCK DIAGRAM

- From the background fabric,
  cut: eight 2½-inch (6.5-cm)
  squares, three 3½-inch
  (9-cm) squares, and four
  3½ × 6½ inch (9 × 16.5 cm)
  rectangles.
- From the small star fabric,
  cut: one 2½-inch (6.5-cm)
  square and four 3½-inch
  (9-cm) squares. Cut each of
  the 3½-inch (9-cm) squares
  once on the diagonal to form
  eight triangles.
- From the large star fabric,
  cut: one 3½-inch (9-cm)
  square and four 4½-inch
  (11.5-cm) squares. Cut each
  of the 4½-inch (11.5-cm)
  squares once on the diagonal
  to form eight triangles.
Star-point triangles can also be
cut from scrap fabric.

Fix-it

FINDING YOUR IMPROV STYLE

Part of the joy (and challenge) of improvisational quilt-
making is getting to "play," and not having to follow a
strict pattern or set of rules. Many "improv" blocks take
shape as you go, without a clear size or pattern as the
goal. If something is too large, cut it off; if it's not big
enough, add another strip. If you "mess up" and what
you're working on doesn't come out quite as you
wanted, try to reconfigure it into something new,
instead of tossing it back into the scrap bin. Beautiful
creations can come from happy accidents or rescued
orphan blocks.

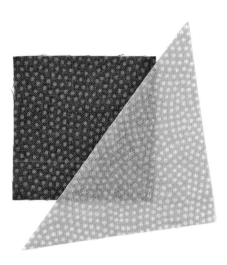

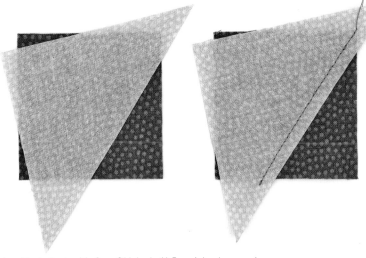

In this block, first we will make an improvisational star that measures 6½ inches (16.5 cm). This star then becomes part of the background for the second star, see the Block Diagram (left). The star points for both stars are constructed in the same manner.

First start with four 2½-inch (6.5-cm) background squares. Place a triangle in the first star fabric over the lower right corner at the angle you want the star point to have. Then carefully flip that triangle 180 degrees and slightly toward the bottom right. Hold or pin it in place and stitch a ¼-inch (6-mm) seam from the edge of the triangle fabric.

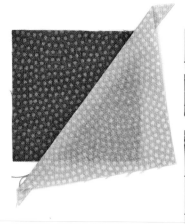

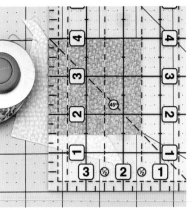

2 Repeat Step 1 to complete four squares. Flip the triangles over and press the units. Trim to 2½ inches (6.5 cm) square—trim from the back, using the background square as a guide. This "sew and flip" method might take some practice, so go ahead and cut a few extra background squares and keep going until you feel comfortable with the technique.

3 Take the remaining four triangles of the first (small) star fabric and place, pin, and sew the second star points on the bottom left corners. Flip, press, and trim as before.

4 Lay out the nine patches and chain piece into a star shape. Follow the instructions for chain piecing on pages 56–59.

5 Now let's move on to the second (larger) star. Take two 3½-inch (9-cm) background squares, two background rectangles, and eight triangles from the second star fabric. Make star points as before, following Steps 1–3. With the rectangles, you can make the points long and skinny for variety.

6 Next, assemble the block in two halves, first joining one star point rectangle to a background rectangle, and then to the first star block. Then join the six pieces of the second star.

7 Join up the center seam and press the seams to one side with a hot iron. Step back and enjoy!

Wth a light fabric as the background and bold colored stars, this mini quilt really stands out!

This improv block is called
"AINU-INSPIRED FREEHAND SPIRAL"

FABRICS

2 fabrics: 1 light background fabric and 1 dark focus fabric for the spiral

EQUIPMENT

• Pins
• Basting thread
• Pencil
• Scissors
• Hand-appliqué tools: thimble, needle, thread

Freehand spiral

I once spent a weekend learning traditional Japanese Ainu appliqué and embroidery with a shopkeeper in Sapporo, Japan. Here is an Ainu-inspired freehand spiral for you to try. It may be hard to cut a shape you're happy with on the first try, so sketch out a bunch of spirals you like before you pick up your scissors. There are no templates for this block; the shapes need to come from inside you.

BLOCK DIAGRAM

• Cut one 13-inch (33-cm) square from the background fabric.
• Cut one 11-inch (28-cm) square from the focus fabric.

On the design wall

Try mirrored or upside-down images (see far left). Alternate with "Rail Fence" (see left and pages 52–55) or "Trip Around the World" (see pages 56–59). No two freehand spiral blocks will be exactly alike, so make a bunch and play around with them. Try some small ones, or tall skinny ones—see which shapes appeal the most.

1 Practice drawing some freehand spirals before you start cutting.

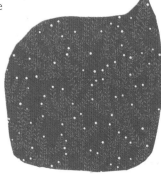

2 Take your 11-inch (28-cm) square of dark focus fabric and cut a shape from it that is not completely round or oval, leaving it pointy in one corner.

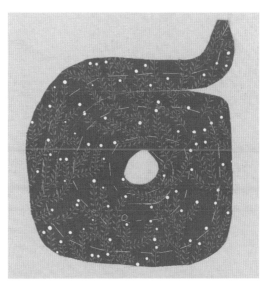

3 Cut along one side of the point, making a tail. Continue to cut a spiral, trying to keep the spacing even as you go.

4 In the center, cut out a small circle. Lay this piece carefully on top of your 13-inch (33-cm) background square. Thread-baste along the center of the spiral.

INSPIRATION IS EVERYWHERE

I was admiring this beautiful Ainu Spiral bag in a shop when I asked the shopkeeper where one would go to learn such a skill. She told me to sit with her and for the next day and a half she taught me the beginnings of what she knew. Chance meetings and simple questions can often lead the way to the best types of learning.

As you whipstitch the top fabric to the bottom fabric, turn ⅛ inch (3 mm) of the raw edge under to expose the background and form your pattern.

5 Start on the inner side of the outermost loop and begin needleturn appliqué. Turn to pages 42–43 for more detailed instructions on this technique. Appliqué all the way around the inside and then the outside of the spiral.

6 Remove the basting threads, press, and then trim the block to a 12½-inch (31.5-cm) square.

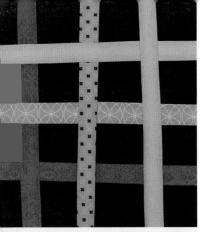

This improv block is called
"RIBBON BLOCK"

FABRICS

1 background fabric and up to 6 different colored fabrics for the strips

EQUIPMENT

• Pins
• Acrylic ruler
• Rotary cutter
• Iron

IMPROV
Slicing and inserting

When you start to let go and play around more with improvisational piecing, sooner or later you stop adding onto your patches, but instead slice into them and insert other fabrics. This block starts with one square that is sliced and a thin ribbon of fabric is inserted into the space. The block is then rotated and the process is repeated until you've got it just the way you want it.

On the design wall

Use several of the same block together to create a "wonky basketweave" illusion (see below left). Alternate with "54–40 or Fight" for a modern look (see below right and pages 74–77).

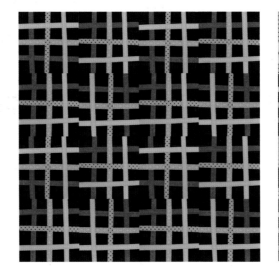

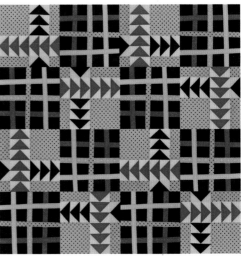

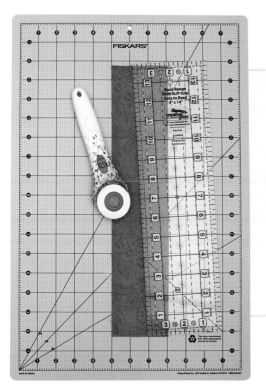

OFF THE STRAIGHT AND NARROW

Part of the fun of improvisational piecing is using patches and strips that aren't exactly rectangular or square in shape. For this block, try cutting a wonky strip. Take a 3- × 14-inch (7.5- × 35.5-cm) strip and place your acrylic ruler in the center, lengthwise along the strip. Skew it slightly so that the strip will be cut in half-ish, not exactly down the 1½-inch (3.8-cm) center point. The angles and volume of color that this technique adds to your block gives the quilt a lot of personality. However you end up cutting your strips, remember to sew with a ¼-inch (6-mm) seam and go for it. Trust your gut.

1 Start with a 12-inch (30.5-cm) square of background fabric. Make a slice all the way across with the acrylic ruler and rotary cutter, about ¼–⅓ of the way down from the top of the square. It doesn't need to be parallel to the top and bottom.

2 Insert a colored strip in the opening and stitch the background pieces to either side. Press toward the background fabric.

3 Turn the block 90 degrees, slice again and insert the second strip. Because you are cutting your sewing lines, backstitch over every intersecting seam to reinforce them.

4 Turn the block 90 degrees again, slice, and insert the third strip. When your slice is not perpendicular to the strip you've cut, you'll need to adjust your fabric a bit to one side in order to get the cut strip to line up with itself. Carefully place the top portion on the new strip and fold it upward, holding about ¼ inch (6 mm) down with your fingers. You can sneak a peek to see if the strips line up or not before pinning and stitching the top portion into place.

5 Continue in this way until all six strips are inserted.

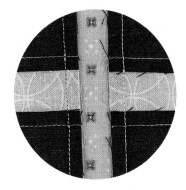

6 Trim the block to 12½ inches (31.5 cm) square to finish.

This improv block is called
"IMPROV HOUSETOP"

FABRICS

4–5 fabrics: any color combination, but aim for some good contrast

EQUIPMENT

• Acrylic ruler
• Rotary cutter
• Pins
• Iron

Slicing and rotating

Sometimes when doing improvisational work, it feels good to just build up a block. Start with a square and add rings around it. It doesn't matter if these rings are not equal or even straight—I often just grab strips from my scrap fabric basket and add rings until the block gets to the desired size (trust your gut). If you can sew a straight ¼-inch (6-mm) seam and you press the block after each addition, it should lay flat. Let some creative freedom come in, grab a rotary cutter, and cut the block into four equal-ish squares. Rotate them and sew them back together. You have created an improv housetop block!

BLOCK DIAGRAM

• Cut one 4-inch (10-cm) square in fabric A.
• Cut strips of all your other fabrics somewhere between 1½ inches (3.8 cm) and 2½ inches (6.5 cm) wide.

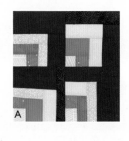

On the design wall

Use several of the same block together for a powerful design. Play around with the rotation of the blocks to see what effects you create (see below left). Try using several of this block surrounding a group of four or nine blocks, such as "Dresden Plate" (see pages 88–91) or "Inside My Heart" (see below right and pages 92–95).

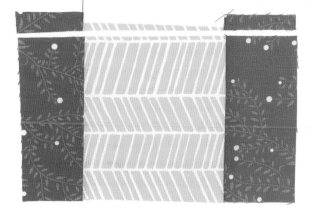

1 Take the 4-inch (10-cm) square of fabric A and use it as a guide to cut two strips from your first ring fabric. Pin them on opposite sides of the square and stitch with a ¼-inch (6-mm) seam, right sides together.

2 Open and press the seams away from the center square. Use your rotary cutter and acrylic ruler to make a straight edge along both sides.

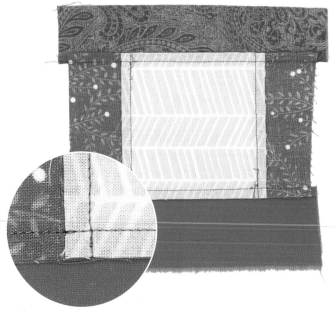

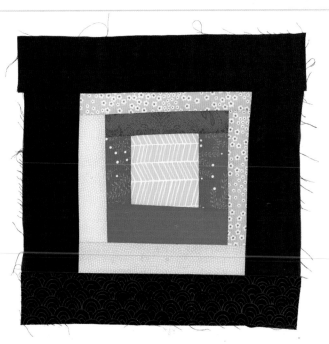

3 Then use the pressed unit to cut two more strips from the first ring fabric. Add these to opposite sides of the piece and once again press the seams away from the center square.

4 Trim up the edges of the unit and continue adding rings in the same manner until your block is about 14 inches (35.5 cm) square. Use ¼-inch (6-mm) seams throughout and always trim a straight edge before adding the next strip. Other than that, don't worry too much about measuring or the width of strips. Even opposite sides of a ring do not need to be exactly the same width.

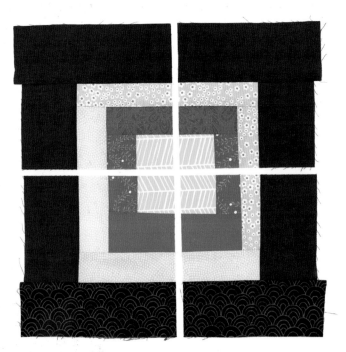

Hints and tips

CREATE A BETTER BLOCK

- As you build with uneven strips, try to compensate for angled pieces with alternate angles on the next round. This will stop your block from turning into a sharp trapezoid and give you a more or less squarish shape to work with.

- Try to make your last ring thicker than the others; this will give you more wiggle room to trim up the block in Step 4.

- If you decide to make an entire quilt of this block (or use several of them in one project), don't join them into 12½-inch (31.5-cm) blocks until later in the project and swap out units so there is more variety in each block. This is a great block to use up scraps!

5 Once your block is about 14 inches (35.5 cm) square, take your rotary cutter and acrylic ruler and make a cut through the center of the block. Then cut the units in half again. Aim for cuts that are 90 degrees to each other.

6 Trim each unit to a 6½-inch (16.5-cm) square. It's okay to skew the blocks slightly; don't try to line up the strip seams with the ruler marks.

7 Lay out the units with the center block color (fabric A) in each one to the lower left. Join the units into a finished block.

Let your fabric and color choices echo throughout a piece made of several blocks, as they do in this mini quilt.

This improv block is called
"IMPROV STRINGS"

FABRICS

Strings or strips of fabric
separated into lights and darks.
The more variety the better.

EQUIPMENT

- Four 6½-inch (16.5-cm) squares
  of thin paper (such as newsprint
  or tracing paper).
- Pencil
- Acrylic ruler
- Pins
- Iron
- Rotary cutter

IMPROV

Improvisational string piecing

String quilts have always been one of my favorite
patterns. There is something about the uneven
widths, irregular angles, and multitude of different
fabrics that, to me, feels like the very heart of
quilt-making. Limit your fabric choices and you
can have a very controlled block. Or grab
anything you can find and make it a free-for-all.
The piecing method is the same—start with a
piece of paper and stitch the fabrics together
using the paper as a foundation. Trim up your
block and remove the paper at the end and you
have tamed some of that string chaos. Repeat a
few times to make a block, or keep going and
create an entire quilt.

BLOCK DIAGRAM

If you are cutting your fabric
strings from yardage, they
should each be 1–2 inches
(2.5–5 cm) wide.

On the design wall

Place several of the same block together and the outer corners will match up to form a diagonal
checkerboard pattern (see below left). For a different look, alternate with "Hawaiian Appliqué
Block" (see below right and pages 96–99) or "English Paper Pieced Hexagon Star" (see pages
102–105). This block also looks great with thin or thick sashing in a bold contrasting color.

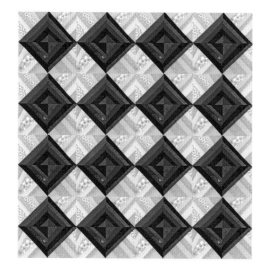

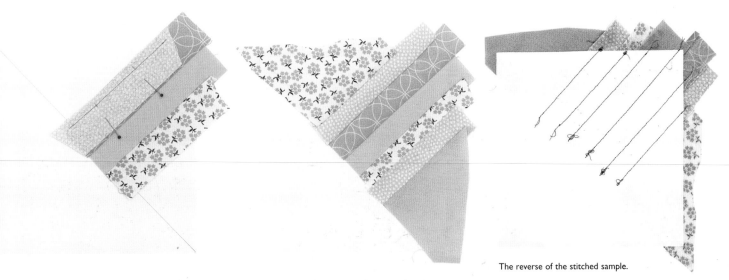

1   Start by drawing a diagonal line across each of your four paper foundation squares. Draw a second line from the center of the square out to a third corner.

2   Work with the short side strings first. Take two light-colored strings, place them right sides together and pin them to the foundation paper, starting about ¼–½ inch (6–13 mm) over the marked center line. These raw edges will be covered by another fabric in a later step.

3   Lower your sewing machine's stitch length to 15spi (1.7 mm) or around there. A shorter stitch length will make it easier to remove the papers later. Stitch along one side of these strings, sewing through the paper, with a ¼-inch (6-mm) seam. Make sure to backstitch at the beginning and end of the strip.

The reverse of the stitched sample.

4   Open the fabrics and lightly press with a dry iron. Align two strings on either end of the stitched pieces and pin them into place. Stitch with a ¼-inch (6-mm) seam as before.

5   Continue adding light-colored strings until the paper foundation is completely covered. It is helpful to pin each string and press them open in turn to avoid puckers and excess fabric in the block.

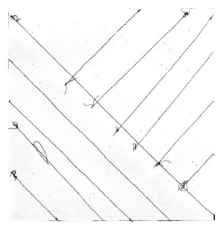

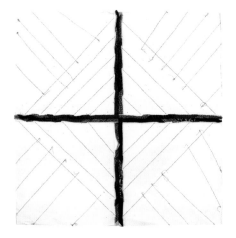

6 Take your first dark-colored string and pin it across the raw edges of all the light strings. Stitch into place. Your sewing line should follow the original pencil markings on the paper, or corner to corner.

7 Press, pin, and sew more dark strings parallel to this one until the block is completely covered. Flip the block over and trim off the excess fabric with your acrylic ruler and rotary cutter. Use the foundation paper as a guide.

8 Repeat Steps 1–7 three more times to make four units. Arrange as in the Block Diagram on page 120 and stitch them together. Press seams open.

REMOVING PAPER FOUNDATIONS

Improvisational foundation paper piecing is an excellent way to use up very small scraps of fabric, and build a block quickly, but at the end, all that paper needs to be torn away. If you keep a short stitch length and tear slowly, the papers should come off easily. First run a fingernail over the seam to perforate one line. Fold the paper back along the next seam and, while putting pressure along the seam line, gently tear away one strip at a time, pulling upward. It is best to wait to remove papers until the blocks are joined into the quilt top. If you plan on making the Skill-Builder Sampler Quilt on pages 142–145, remove the foundation papers after the top is completely assembled.

9 Follow the instructions in the box at left to remove all the paper foundations once the block has been sewn into your quilt top. Removing the foundation paper early may result in the edges of the block stretching out of shape.

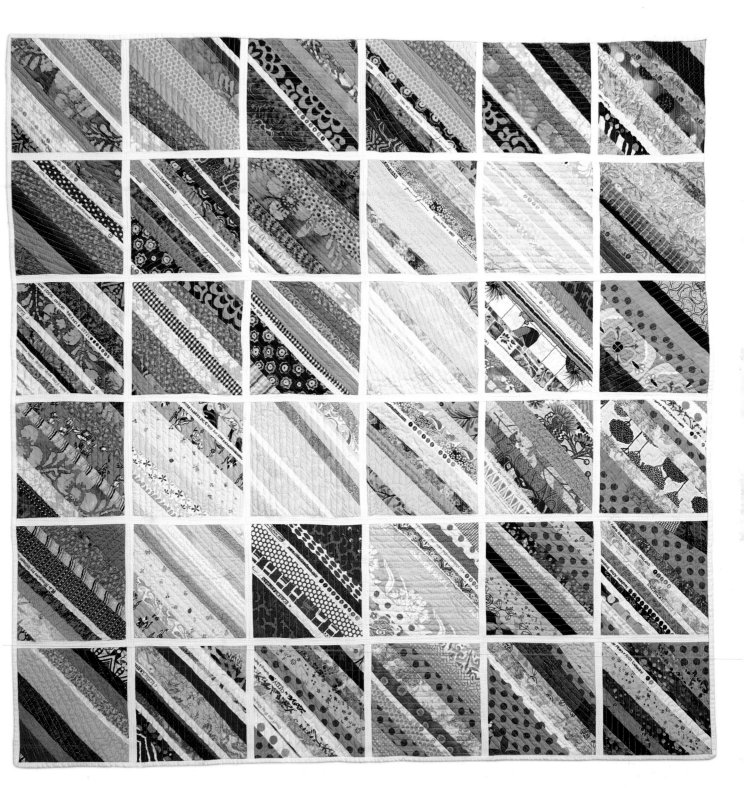

If your scraps and strings overwhelm you, try
sorting them and piecing blocks by color.
Color-block quilts in a straight setting can
give scrappy chaos a harmonious feel.

This improv block is called
"MIXED-TECHNIQUE BASKET"

FABRICS

6–9 assorted fabrics for the
basket body
1 strip of bias fabric in a similar
shade to the basket fabrics for
the handle
Contrasting fabric for the
background

EQUIPMENT

• Pins
• Acrylic ruler
• Self-healing cutting mat
• Rotary cutter
• Iron

IMPROV

Free-cut curves

By now you should feel pretty confident in your
basic quilting skills. You know how to follow
rules; you know how to break them. As long as
your block is well constructed, give yourself all
the creative freedom you need to express what
you want in fabric. In this block we mix
techniques to make an improvisational version
of a basket, one of the more traditional motifs
in historical quilts.

While the instructions that follow will guide
you to make a block similar to the one in the
top-left corner, if you end up with something
completely different, that's more than ok.
The example block uses a nine-patch square as
the basket body, but you could also try a free-
pieced or string-pieced patch, an improv star, or
an orphan block left over from another project.
Play around and see what you can make.

BLOCK DIAGRAM

• Cut a total of nine 2¾-inch
  (7-cm) squares for the basket
  body from 6–9 fabrics.
• Cut a 14- × 1¼-inch (35.5- ×
  3.2-cm) strip of bias binding
  for the handle.
• From the background fabric,
  cut: one top rectangle, 13 × 6
  inches (33 × 15 cm), one
  center rectangle, 11 × 5½
  inches (28 × 14 cm), one
  bottom rectangle, 13 × 2½
  inches (33 × 6.5 cm).

GIVING NEW LIFE TO ORPHAN BLOCKS

Often we try a new block or make several blocks/units
for a project and end up with extras, mistake blocks
that don't measure up, or ones we just don't like in the
finished layout. These blocks get tossed into a pile of
"orphans" and patiently wait for a new life. This basket
block is a great place to give these tossed-aside pieces
a new purpose. Try adding any of your cast-offs in
place of the nine-patch center and see what personality
your baskets can gain.

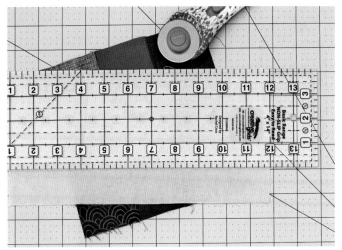

1 | Make a nine-patch block from the assorted 2¾-inch (7-cm) fabric squares (see pages 56–59 for details on how to do this).

2 | Place your nine-patch block slightly skewed on the cutting mat. Lay the center background strip on top and use an acrylic ruler to cut the nine-patch block to size.

3 | Carefully place the nine-patch block on top of the center background strip, with about 4 inches (10 cm) of the background fabric showing from the top right corner of the basket fabric. With a rotary cutter, cut a curve to make the right side of the basket, through both the nine-patch block and the background strip.

4 | Remove the excess portion of the nine-patch block and carefully flip the background piece on top of the basket body. Using lots of pins, join and piece this curve carefully. Press the seam to one side.

5 | Return to the cutting mat to make the other side of the basket. Align the straight edge of the sewn piece with one of the lines on your cutting mat. Take the loose background strip and place it on a line about 13½ inches (34.5 cm) away from the first. Place the basket fabric on top of the background strip to be cut and cut a curve to make the second side of the basket. Pin and piece the fabric as before. Press whichever way allows the seam to lie flatter

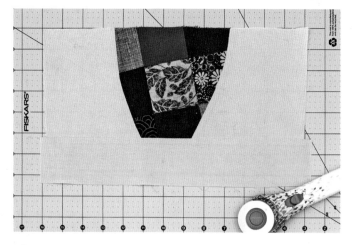

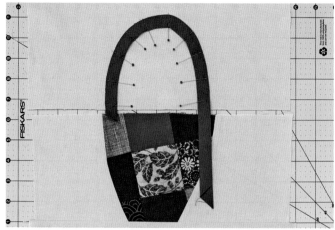

6 Trim up both top and bottom basket edges, then pin and sew the bottom background strip to the bottom edge of your basket section. It is ok if the edges of the block don't match up at this stage, as they will be trimmed down later.

7 Make sure your bias binding strip is at least 14 inches (35.5 cm) long (see pages 39–40 for instructions on making bias strips). Pin into place on to the top background strip, aligning the edges so that they will be positioned just inside the basket edges.

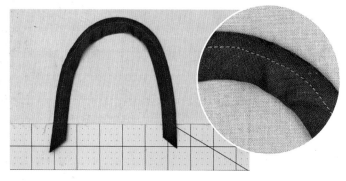

8 Machine-stitch ¼ inch (6 mm) away from the raw edge of the handle strip.

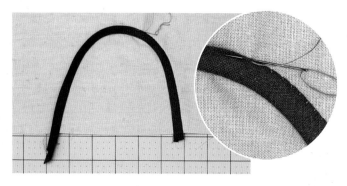

9 Press the folded edge over and whipstitch appliqué the strip into place.

10 Align the two sides of the handle with the basket edges and machine-stitch the background strip with the handle on to the rest of the block. Press the seam away from the basket and trim the block to a 12½-inch (31.5-cm) square.

Once you start making baskets,
it can be hard to stop!

CHAPTER 3
Quilting Projects

STRING PILLOW • SEWING-MACHINE COVER • DRESDEN TABLE RUNNER
SKILL-BUILDER SAMPLER QUILT • DOLL QUILT AND PILLOW

Projects
String pillow

Savor all of your precious scraps in this cheerful pillow. The more fabrics you can use, the better here! This project uses the same block pattern as on pages 120–123, but the units have been adjusted to 8 inches (20.5 cm) and it finishes at 16 inches (40.5 cm) square.

Dimensions

16 × 16 inches
(40.5 × 40.5 cm)

Fabrics

Assorted scrap fabrics in strips or strings, separated into brights and neutrals (the equivalent of 8–12 fat eighths)
Two pieces of fabric for the pillow back, 16½ × 12 inches (42 × 30.5 cm) each

Equipment and Other Materials

• Thin paper or newsprint
• 20-inch (51-cm) square piece of batting
• 20-inch (51-cm) square piece of lining fabric
• 2- × 7-inch (5- × 18-cm) piece of fusible interfacing
• Spray baste
• 2 buttons
• 2 small hair elastics
• 75 inches (190.5 cm) of binding, cut 2¼ inches (5.5 cm) wide
• Thread for piecing, thicker thread for attaching the buttons
• 16-inch (40.5 cm) pillow form

1 Cut out four squares measuring 8½ × 8½ inches (21.5 × 21.5 cm) from thin paper such as newsprint.

2 Follow Steps 1–6 on pages 121–122 to make the string blocks, then stitch them together to make a 16½-inch (42-cm) square. Press the seams open.

Pressing seams open will eliminate a bulky center and make the pillow easier to quilt.

3 Carefully begin to remove the foundation papers. Press along the seam with your fingernail to loosen it slightly before tearing.

4 Be careful not to pull or distort any of the stitches.

5 Carefully remove the foundation paper from the seam allowance. A pair of tweezers might be helpful here. Give the top a good press.

6 Layer your top, batting, and lining fabrics, and spray baste. You can use muslin for the lining fabric, or any fabric you're trying to use up.

7 Quilt as desired.

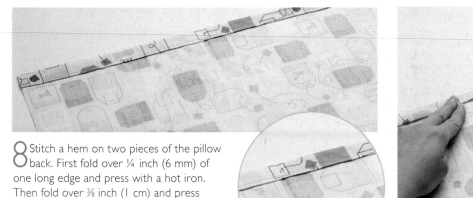

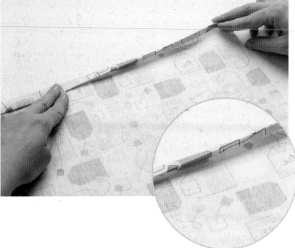

8 Stitch a hem on two pieces of the pillow back. First fold over ¼ inch (6 mm) of one long edge and press with a hot iron. Then fold over ⅜ inch (1 cm) and press again before top-stitching by machine.

9 Layer the backing pieces on the wrong side of the quilted piece and mark where the buttons and hair elastics will go.

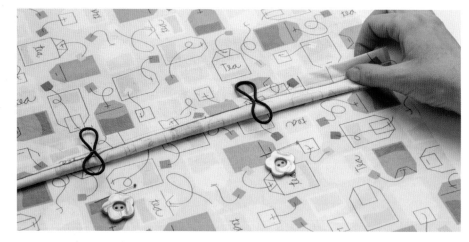

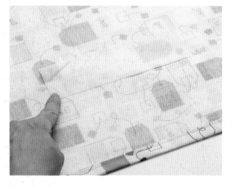

10 Iron the interfacing strip horizontally on the wrong side of the lower backing piece, behind where the buttons will go.

11 Attach the buttons by hand and attach the hair elastics by machine.

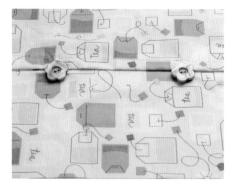

12 Reposition the backing fabrics on the wrong side of the pillow top and pin into place.

13 Pin the binding to the front of the quilted piece. Attach the binding by machine, assembling the pillow back at the same time. Take care to backstitch at the openings of the pillow back. Remove the pins and attach the binding to the pillow back by hand.

14 Stuff the finished pillow case with the pillow form and enjoy.

Projects
Sewing-machine cover

Protect your sewing machine from dust and brighten up your sewing area at the same time. Let these big, bold flying geese encourage you to spend more time at the machine. This project uses the same block units as on pages 70–73 but they have been enlarged to be 2½- × 5-inch (6.5- × 12.5-cm) finished geese. After measuring your sewing machine, adjust the number of geese in the vertical row and the dimensions of the background fabric for a perfect fit.

Dimensions

15½ × 30 inches
(39.5 × 76 cm)

Fabrics

18 inches (45.75 cm) of fabric for the background
18 inches (45.75 cm) of light colored fabric for the "sky" portion of the geese blocks
18 inches (45.75 cm) of 4–6 assorted fabrics for the "geese"

Equipment and Other Materials

• 84 inches (2.1 m) of grosgrain ribbon, cut into four 21-inch (53.5-cm) pieces for the ties
• 19- × 34-inch (48.5- × 86.5-cm) piece of batting
• 19- × 34-inch (48.5- × 86.5-cm) piece of backing fabric
• 2¾ yards (2.5 m) of bias binding, cut 2¼ inches (5.5 cm) wide

MEASURE YOUR MACHINE

Take a measuring tape and, starting at the bottom of the front of your machine, measure up, over, and down the other side. This is your length. Now measure across the front of the machine at the widest part— this is your width. Use these dimensions to plan the finished size of your project.

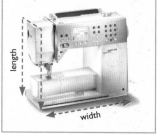

length

width

Following Steps 1–5 on pages 71–72, piece and trim as many geese units as you need to total the length of the machine cover. For example, this cover is 30 inches (76 cm) long, so 12 geese were used. For variety, piece geese of several colors and arrange them as you like. You may find you have leftover geese units, but set them aside for a future project.

CUTTING

• From the background fabric, cut: one strip, 2¾ × 30 inches (7 × 76 cm) and one strip 8¼ × 30 inches (21 × 76 cm).
• Cut 6¼-inch (16-cm) squares from the "goose" fabrics (each square makes 4 geese).
• Cut four 3⅜-inch (8.5-cm) squares from the "sky" fabric for each large goose square.

3 Layer and spray baste the top, batting, and backing fabrics (refer to pages 36–37 for details on how to do this).

2 Place the background fabric strips on either side of the row of geese. Press away from the geese strip.

4 Hand- or machine-quilt.

5 Pin the binding into place. Before stitching down your binding, attach the grosgrain ribbons 6 inches (15 cm) from the bottom of each side.

6 As you bind the quilt, the ribbons will get secured. Add a label (see page 41) and try the cover on your machine.

Projects
Dresden table runner

There is something really sweet about shrinking standard blocks down to tiny versions. This Dresden runner has been made using the same construction as the "Dresden Plate" block (see pages 88–91), but the petals have been reduced to fit onto a 9-inch (23-cm) block. Put five blocks in a row, turn them on point, and you're ready for spring (or any season) with this sweet and quick-to-make table runner.

Dimensions

12 × 64½ inches
(30.5 × 164 cm)

Fabrics

Assorted pink fabrics totaling 8–12 fat eighths (each block uses four different fabrics)

Five 3⅝-inch (9-cm) squares of green fabric for the Dresden centers

Five 10-inch (25.5-cm) squares of background fabric (can be cut from ½ yard/45 cm of fabric)

Four 9⅞-inch (25.2-cm) squares cut once on the diagonal to make four setting triangles (can be cut from ½ yard/45 cm of fabric)

Equipment and Other Materials

- 14- × 68-inch (35.5- × 172.5-cm) piece of batting
- 15- × 68-inch (38- × 172.5-cm) piece of backing fabric (this can be pieced from a one-yard cut)
- Spray baste
- 182 inches (4.62 m) of binding, cut 2¼ inches (5.5 cm) wide
- Hand-appliqué supplies: thimble, needle, thread
- Templates on page 155

Using the "Dresden Table Runner" templates on page 152, cut 60 petals from the assorted pink fabrics.

2 Baste the green squares around five hexagons. See Basics of English Paper Piecing on pages 44–45 for details on how to do this.

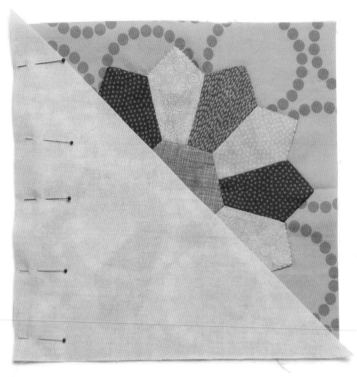

3 Following the directions on pages 88–91, join the petals into rings and complete five Dresden blocks.

4 Carefully stitch setting triangles onto opposite corners of the center Dresden blocks, following the diagram on page 140.

BLOCK JOINING SEQUENCE

Follow this diagram to connect the triangles and Dresden blocks in Step 4.

5 Press the triangles away from the Dresden blocks. Pin units carefully, butting seams, and join into a row.

6 Layer your top, batting, and lining fabrics, and spray baste.

7 Quilt the table runner as desired.

8 Trim any excess batting and backing, and bind following the instructions on pages 36–37 and 39–40. When folding the binding for the 135-degree angle, be sure to align the strip with the next edge when you fold back, not into a 45-degree fold as with a quilt corner. Enjoy!

Projects

Skill-builder sampler quilt

Do you want to show off your new quilting skills? Do you like to work with a clear goal in mind to keep your motivation up? Then this project is the one for you. It uses 20 12½-inch (31.5-cm) (unfinished) blocks and 3-inch (7.5-cm) sashing strips to make a twin-bed-sized quilt full of fun and memories of your quilting journey. Choose any 20 of the technique blocks demonstrated in the previous chapter and put them together to show off and enjoy. Years from now you can look back and laugh at your fabric choices, and then smile at how far you've come.

Dimensions

66 × 81 inches (1.67 × 2 m)

Fabrics

20 completed blocks of your choice from Chapter 2 (pages 52–127)—see fabric requirements for each block

4¾ yards (4.3 m) of solid fabric for the sashing strips and border. (This measurement assumes that long border strips are not pieced.)

5¾ yards (5.25 m) of fabric for the backing. Piece with a vertical seam

Equipment and Other Materials

• 76- × 91-inch (1.9- × 2.3-m) piece of batting (twin- or full-sized pre-packaged batting should work)

• 8½ yards (7.75 m) of bias binding, cut 2¼ inches (5.5 cm) wide

• Fabric and marking pen to make your label

• Extra backing fabric to make a hanging sleeve, if needed

CUTTING

From the 4¾ yards (4.3 m) of border/sashing fabric, cut: four strips 4½ inches (11.5 cm) wide for the border (we will trim these to size later), four strips 3½ × 57½ inches (9 × 146 cm) for the horizontal sashing, and 15 strips 3½ × 12½ (9 × 31.5 cm) for the vertical sashing.

Make 20 blocks of your choice from the Techniques chapter. Make the blocks you love or want to challenge yourself to complete. If you really enjoy a few techniques, go ahead and make several of those blocks and add them in to your total 20. Square all the blocks up to 12½ inches (31.5 cm). Throw them up on your design wall and make sure you're happy (see the panel on page 143) before moving onto Step 2—be patient.

2 Once you're sure about the design of your quilt you can move on. Starting with the top row, pin and sew a vertical sashing strip between each block. Press toward the sashing strips. Repeat for all 5 rows.

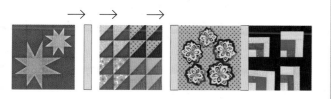

GETTING YOUR LAYOUT RIGHT

Throw them up on your design wall (or design bed or design floor—whatever space works for you) and space them about 3 inches (7.5 cm) apart. Play around with the arrangement until you find something that you like. There are no hard-and-fast rules to this part—put the blocks where you like them. Step back and look at them for a while. Take off your glasses. Take a photo with your phone or digital camera so you can see the entire quilt in a smaller frame. Colors or shapes/lines that pop out unattractively should be moved until it feels "right" to you. I like to leave the blocks up on the wall for a few days and glance up at them as I walk past. You'll know when it's ready to be sewn together.

3 Again starting with the top row, pin and sew a horizontal sashing strip between each row. First find and crease the center of the sashing strip and the center of the block row (fold in half and pinch). Align the centers and pin from this point outward toward each end. Sew long seams slowly, taking backstitches at each seam you cross (sashing and block seams) to reinforce them. Press each long seam toward the sashing strip.

4 Lay the quilt top out on the floor or a large table and, with a measuring tape, measure from the top to the bottom edge, through the center of the quilt (see page 35). This is the measurement you will use for the length of your first (side) border strips.

5 Fold the border strips in half and find the center. Fold the quilt top in half and find the center. Align the center marks and pin outward as in Step 3. Sew borders on slowly and take backstitches on crossed seams. Press toward the border.

6 Take a measurement through the center of the quilt top again, this time from side to side (including border strips). This is the measurement you will use for the length of your top and bottom borders. Fold, mark centers, pin and sew as in Step 5. Press toward the borders and you're done with the top!

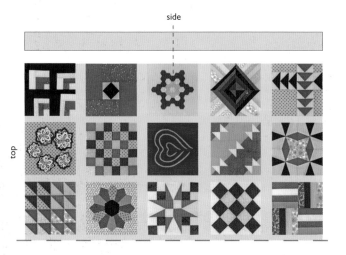

7 Layer and baste following the instructions on pages 36–37. Quilt by hand or machine, or send it to your favorite long-armer.

8 Square up the quilt with your acrylic ruler and rotary cutter. Add binding and a label, toss it in the wash to freshen it up, and enjoy.

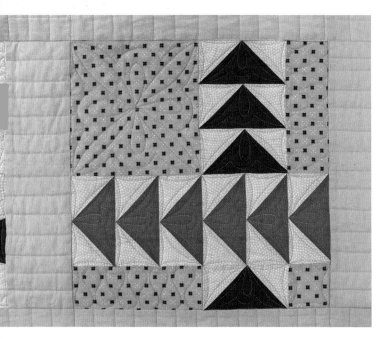

Projects
Doll quilt and pillow

This adorable doll quilt is sharp and sassy with bright zigzags made from equilateral triangles and half hexagons. Use your favorite fabric and why not make a tiny pillow to match?

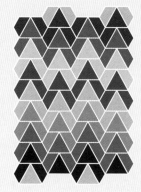

A plan of the quilt top showing how it is constructed using triangles and half hexagons.

Dimensions

Quilt: 14½ × 19½ inches (37 × 49.5 cm)
Pillow: 8 × 5¾ inches (20.5 × 14.5 cm)

Fabrics

For the quilt: assorted fabrics—fat-quarter-friendly
For the pillow: one 6½- × 17½-inch (16.5- × 44.5-cm) piece of neutral fabric and one 7- × 21-inch (18- × 53.5-cm) piece of patterned fabric that co-ordinates with the quilt fabrics

Equipment

• 32 3-inch (7.5-cm) equilateral triangle templates (see page 153)
• 64 1½-inch (3.8-cm) half-hexagon templates (see page 152)
• 70 inches (1.78 m) of bias binding (one fat quarter), cut 2¼ inches (5.5 cm) wide
• 18- × 24-inch (45.5- × 61-cm) piece of batting
• 18- × 24-inch (45.5- × 61-cm) piece of backing fabric
• Rotary cutter
• Acrylic ruler
• Perle cotton (if hand-quilting)
• Hand-sewing kit: needle, thread, paper clips, thread wax, thimble
• Fiberfill or batting scraps
• Pins

To make the quilt

1 Cut and baste the fabrics to your templates. Refer to the Basics of English Paper Piecing on pages 44–45 for help on how to do this. Be sure to baste all templates in the same direction so the seam tails are consistently going in the same direction.

2 Assemble each unit with two half hexagons on either side of a triangle, as shown. Use the diagram above as a guide for color placement. Write the block number on the template paper on the back of each unit to help you keep track.

3 Assemble all the units into four columns of eight units.

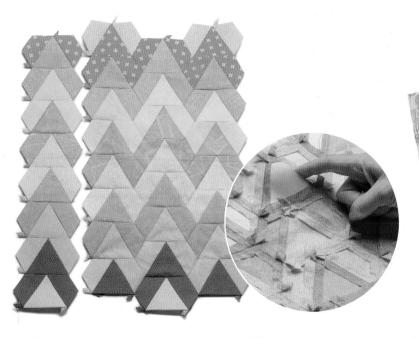

4 Place the four columns side-by-side and join to complete the top.

5 Remove the template papers (see page 45) and give a good press.

6 Layer and spray baste the top, batting, and backing (refer to page 37 for help with this).

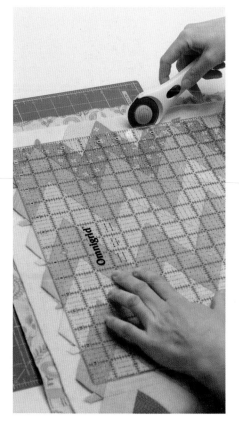

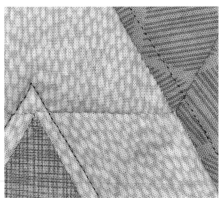

7 Quilt by hand or machine.

8 Square up the top with your rotary cutter and acrylic quilter's ruler. Here we aren't really making a "square." Instead trim to 14½ × 19½ inches (37 × 49.5 cm). Place your rotary cutter just outside of the folded edge of the innermost English paper pieced patches, as shown here, so you don't cut through them.

9 Bind and add your label (see page 41).

To make the pillow

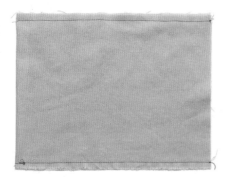

1 Fold the rectangle of neutral fabric in half, right sides together, and stitch down the two long sides, leaving the short side open for turning.

2 Turn right side out and press with a hot iron. Fold under ⅜ inch (1 cm) of the raw edge and press a crease. Stuff with fiberfill or batting scraps. Cut batting scraps into 1–2-inch (2.5–5-cm) squares first, so the pillow is nice and fluffy.

3 Fold in the raw edges, pin, and carefully sew the pillow shut by machine.

4 Take the patterned fabric, fold the narrow edges over twice, press, then topstitch.

5 Fold the piece wrong sides together so that the two ends overlap and the pillowcase length comes to 8 inches (20.5 cm). Sew just under ¼ inch (6 mm) from the top and bottom sides.

6 Flip the pillowcase inside out, press, and stitch the seams again, just over ¼ inch (6 mm) to make a French seam.

7 Turn the pillowcase right side out again and insert your pillow form.

Estimating fabric quantities and math reference

Math for quilting isn't difficult. Use these basic tips as a quick reference when designing and planning your quilt.

Calculating fabric quantities

For a rough idea of how much fabric you need, note down how many blocks you want to make, then the sizes and number of pieces for each fabric. Multiply these together. For example, if you need four 2½ inch (6.4 cm) squares for each block and there are 20 blocks, you will need 80 squares. To cut these in four rows of 20 squares across, 42-inch (106.5-cm) wide fabric would require 15 inches (38.1 cm) of fabric, allowing 15 squares in each row. Add a little extra in case the fabric is cut slightly off the grain and remember you cannot use the selvedges. If the fabric is "fussy cut," selecting a particular motif or stripe direction, you will need more fabric.

Basic patch sizes

These diagrams are a handy quick reference for working out the cutting sizes for half- and quarter-square triangles, 45-degree diamonds, and trapezoids.

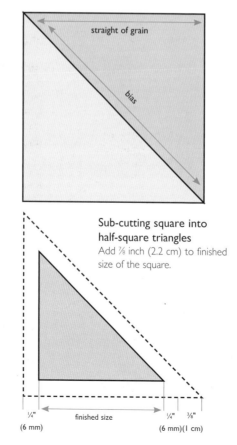

straight of grain

bias

Sub-cutting square into half-square triangles

Add ⅞ inch (2.2 cm) to finished size of the square.

¼" (6 mm)   finished size   ¼" (6 mm) ⅜" (1 cm)

Sub-cutting square into quarter-square triangles

Add 1¼ inch (3.2 cm) to finished size of the square.

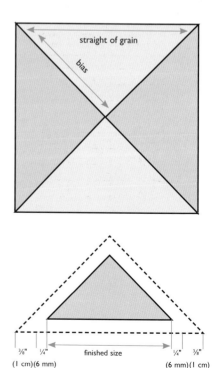

straight of grain

bias

⅜" (1 cm) ¼" (6 mm)   finished size   ¼" (6 mm) ⅜" (1 cm)

Sub-cutting strip into 45-degree diamonds

The width of the strip (a) equals the width between the parallel sides (b). The seam allowance around the shape is ¼ inch (6 mm).

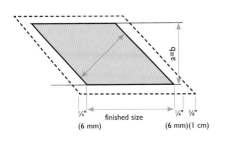

finished size
¼" (6 mm)   ¼" ⅜" (6 mm)(1 cm)

Sub-cutting 45-degree miters

The width of the strip equals the width between the parallel sides.

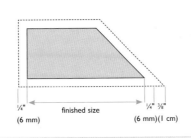

¼" (6 mm)   finished size   ¼" ⅜" (6 mm)(1 cm)

Sub-cutting 45-degree trapezoids

The width of the strip equals the width between the parallel sides.

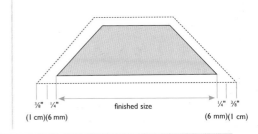

⅜" ¼" (1 cm)(6 mm)   finished size   ¼" ⅜" (6 mm)(1 cm)

Geometry of a square

Useful block sizes

Traditional blocks divide easiest into certain sizes. The table shows the individual square size for each suitable block size (finished sizes). Larger quilts usually look best with larger block sizes. Multiply by 2.54 for metric equivalents.

block size	block type			
	four patch	five patch	seven patch	nine patch
4 in	2 in	x	x	x
5 in	2½ in	1 in	x	x
6 in	3 in	x	x	2 in
7 in	x	x	1 in	x
8 in	4 in	x	x	x
9 in	x	x	x	3 in
10 in	5 in	2 in	x	x
12 in	6 in	x	x	4 in
14 in	x	x	2 in	x
15 in	x	3 in	x	5 in
18 in	4½ in	x	x	6 in

To set blocks on point (diagonally) with plain triangles, work out edge (setting) triangles as follows (finished sizes):

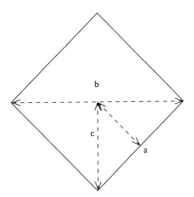

a = side of block
$a^2 = a \times a$
b = side of setting triangle (side)
$c = \frac{1}{2}b$ = side of setting triangle (corners)
$\sqrt{}$ = square root

$2 \times (a^2) = b^2$

$2 \times (b^2) = c^2$

Worked example:

$a = 12$ in
$a^2 = 12 \times 12 = 144$
$2 \times (a^2) = 288 = b^2$
$\sqrt{288} = 16.97 = b$
Round up or down to nearest
1/16 in = 17 in

Remember to add seam allowances!

Use the information below to calculate bed quilt sizes.

Standard bed and quilt sizes

Batting sizes

craft	45 × 36 in (114 × 91 cm)
crib	60 × 45 in (152 × 114 cm)
twin	92 × 72 in (234 × 183 cm)
queen	92 × 108 in (234 × 274 cm)
king	120 × 120 in (305 × 305 cm)

Standard bed mattress sizes (may vary)

crib	46 × 23 in (117 × 58 cm)
twin	75 × 39 in (190 × 99 cm)
full/double	75 × 54 in (190 × 137 cm)
queen	80 × 60 in (203 × 152 cm)
king	80 × 76 in (203 × 193 cm)

Remember:

The quilt center usually corresponds to the mattress size.

Add 12 inches (31 cm) to the length of the center panel (= mattress size) to tuck under pillows, if desired.

Measure the height of the bed, e.g., 18 inches (46 cm) and add this measurement to three sides only.

Bed quilt borders may be on four sides or on three sides only.

Templates

Here you'll find the actual-size templates for use in the techniques and projects. Photocopy the correct number onto paper or cardstock as required.

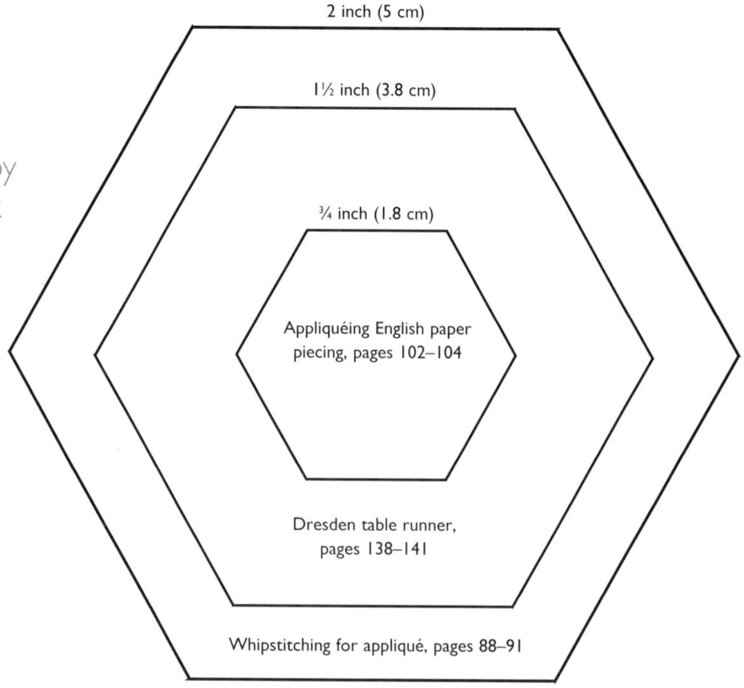

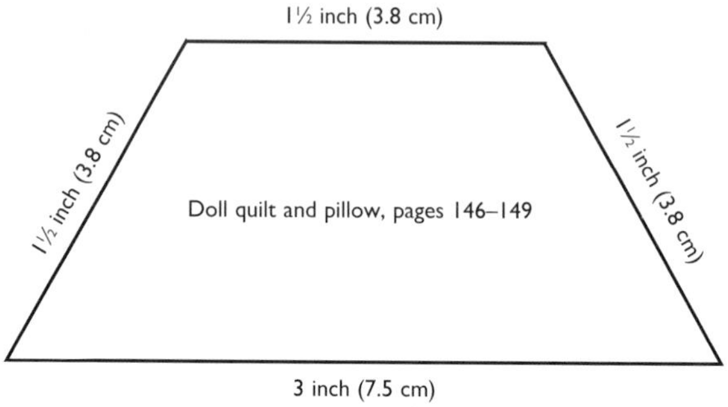

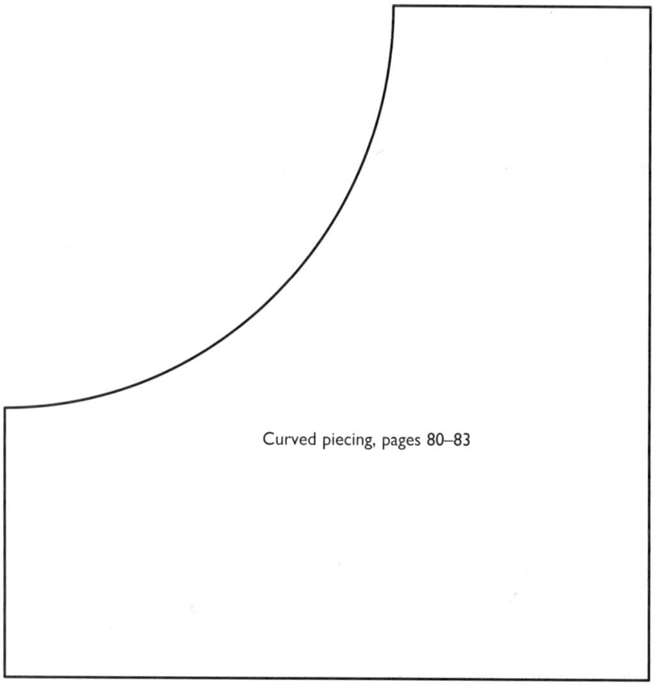

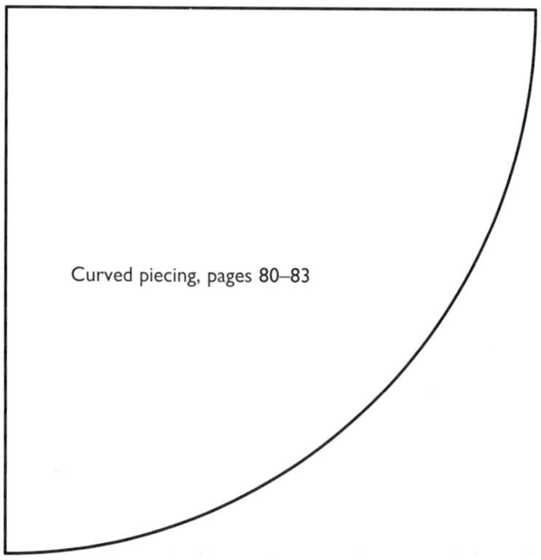

2 inch (5 cm)

1½ inch (3.8 cm)

¾ inch (1.8 cm)

Appliquéing English paper piecing, pages 102–104

Dresden table runner, pages 138–141

Whipstitching for appliqué, pages 88–91

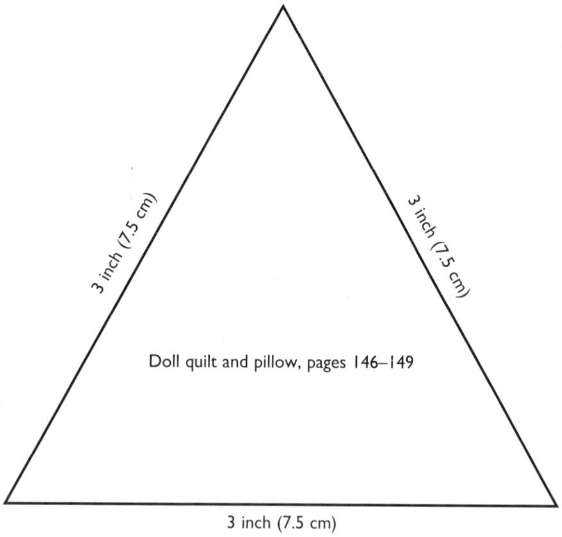

3 inch (7.5 cm)

3 inch (7.5 cm)

Doll quilt and pillow, pages 146–149

3 inch (7.5 cm)

1½ inch (3.8 cm)

1½ inch (3.8 cm)

1½ inch (3.8 cm)

Doll quilt and pillow, pages 146–149

3 inch (7.5 cm)

Curved piecing, pages 80–83

Curved piecing, pages 80–83

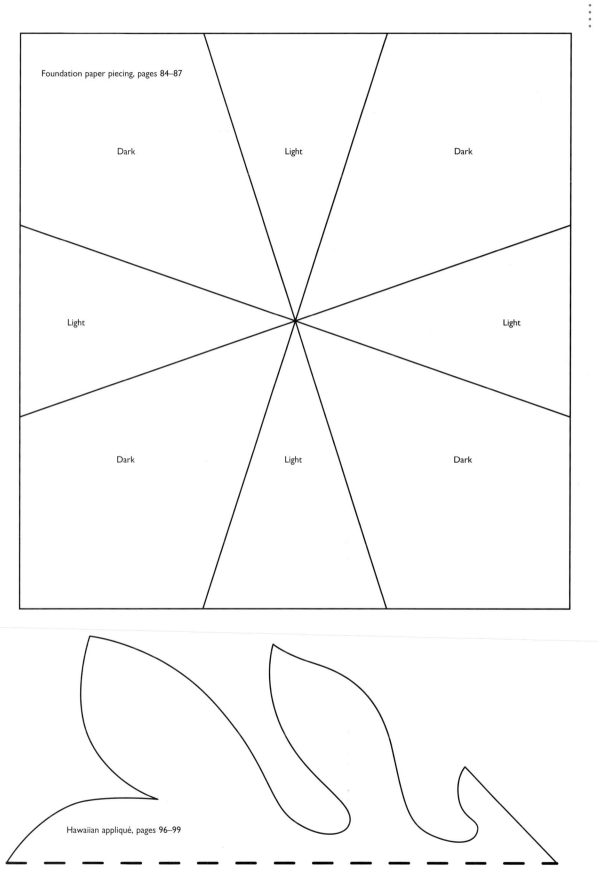

Foundation paper piecing, pages 84–87

Dark	Light	Dark
Light		Light
Dark	Light	Dark

Hawaiian appliqué, pages 96–99

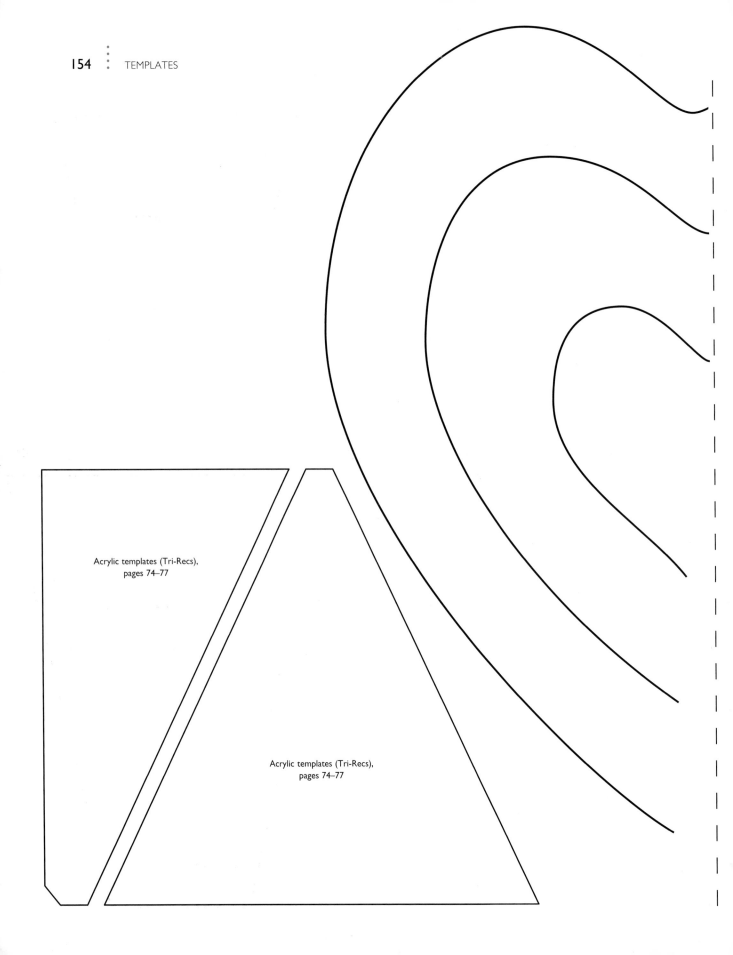

Acrylic templates (Tri-Recs),
pages 74–77

Acrylic templates (Tri-Recs),
pages 74–77

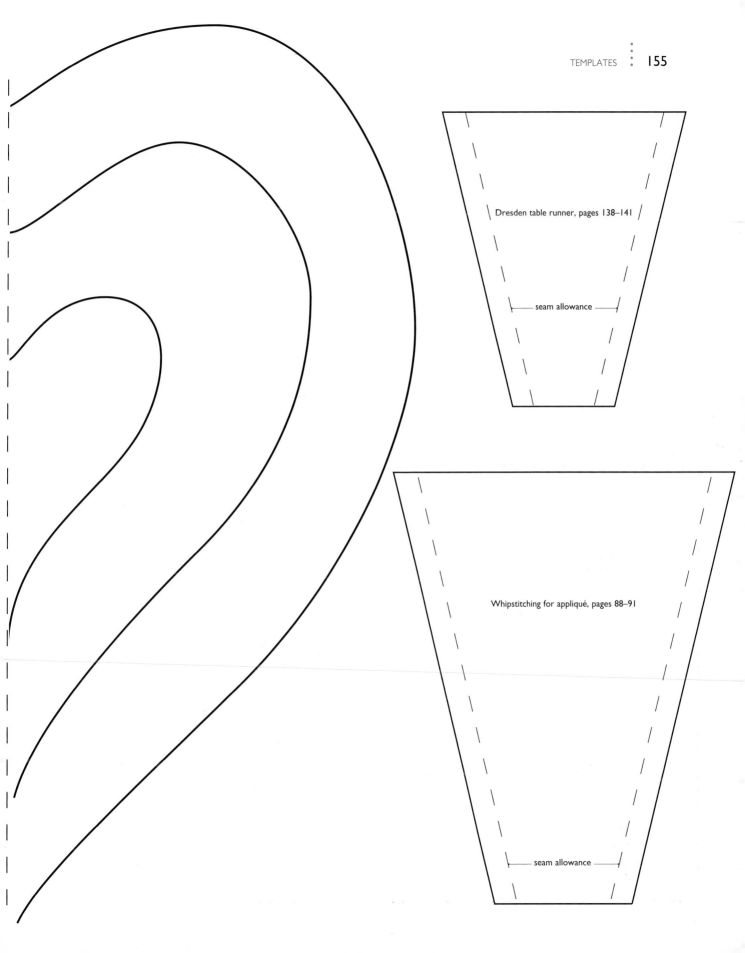

Dresden table runner, pages 138–141

seam allowance

Whipstitching for appliqué, pages 88–91

seam allowance

Glossary

Acrylic quilter's ruler
For cutting your fabric, used with a cutting mat and rotary cutter. Should have clear 45- and 60-degree angle markings.

Appliqué
When one fabric is laid on top and sewn to a background fabric.

Backing fabric
Any fabric used for the back of the quilt.

Backstitch
Sewing where the stitches overlap each other, to make the line of sewing more secure.

Backtack
Sewing over one spot a couple of times to secure your stitches when you start or stop.

Backtrack
Taking a few stitches along the seam allowance on the wrong side of an EPP template to get your needle and thread into position to join the next section. Technique used instead of tying off, clipping your thread, and restarting in a new area.

Basting
Large running stitches used to hold two or more layers in position before final sewing or quilting. Can also be done with safety pins.

Basting spray
Fabric-safe spray adhesive sold in most craft stores, used to hold the layers of a quilt together during the quilting process.

Batting
Soft layer that goes between a quilt top and the backing fabric. Can be made from cotton, bamboo, polyester, and even recycled plastic bottles.

Bias binding
Thin strips of fabric cut on a 45-degree angle and joined to make a continuous piece that is then attached to the front edge of a quilt, folded over, and stitched down to cover the raw edges and finish the project.

Binding
Finishing raw edges around the sides of the quilt by enclosing them in strips of folded fabric.

Broderie Perse
Printed motifs cut out from fabric and used as appliqué pieces.

Chain piecing
Machine sewing patchwork pieces together without cutting the thread between sewn pieces.

EPP (English paper piecing)
Making patchwork by basting fabric over templates, then stitching the seams by hand.

Fat quarter
Yard or meter of fabric quartered equally by cutting down and across.

Foundation piecing
A method of making patchwork sewn to a fabric (permanent) or paper (temporary) backing (the "foundation").

Fussy cutting
Patchwork pieces cut selectively from a printed fabric.

Hanging sleeve
A tube that is sewn to the top-back of a quilt to allow it to be hung and displayed.

Hawaiian appliqué
Traditional symmetrical, linked appliqué motifs, usually large, created like folded paper cuts.

HST
Half-square triangle. Patchwork square made of two equal triangles (also called "triangle square").

Lining fabric/pieces
Fabric that goes on the underside or inside of a project. For example, the inside of a pillow or bag.

Loft (batting)
Height or thickness of a batting.

Long-arm quilting
Stitching on an industrial sewing machine with a wide area under the machine throat, used for professional machine-quilting.

Needleturn appliqué
The point of the sewing needle is used to turn under a narrow hem around the appliqué shape.

Nine patch
Patchwork block with nine main units.

Perlé cotton
Two-ply, non-divisible, twisted cotton thread popular in many forms of needlecraft. Perlé cotton size 8 is used to create big hand-quilted stitches.

Pressing
Using an iron to flatten your quilt after it has been joined together, but before it has been quilted, to make sure the seams fall in the direction you had planned.

QAL (Quilt-along)
Online trend where one person posts an idea, theme, or pattern and invites others to join in and form a group where they can encourage each other and share results as they all work on the same project.

QST
Quarter-square triangle. Patchwork square made of four equal triangles.

Quilt sandwich
Backing, batting, and top quilt layers—the batting is the "filling."

Reverse needleturn appliqué
A hole is cut from the background fabric and the appliqué fabric added from behind but sewn from the front.

Rotary cutter
Cutting tool with a disk blade.

Sashing
Fabric strips set between quilt blocks, usually of a contrasting color.

Scrap quilt
Patchwork made from leftover pieces of other sewing projects.

Seam allowance
Area between the cut edge of fabric and the line of stitching, necessary to stop patchwork from unraveling.

Specialty ruler
Acrylic quilter's ruler sold in shapes specific for cutting one type of fabric patch.

String patchwork
Patchwork made from narrow strips.

Template
Paper, cardboard, or plastic piece used to trace and/or cut out a patchwork shape.

Topstitch
Machine-stitch where the thread is visible from the top side of the finished project.

Whipstitch
Overcast stitch used to join fabric in English paper piecing and appliqué.

Wrap knot
Wrapping the thread around the needle before pulling a stitch through the fabric, so creating a small knot to secure stitches.

Resources

Some of my favorite brick and mortar quilt stores

Portsmouth Fabric Company
www.portsmouthfabric.com
112 Penhallow St.
Portsmouth, NH 03801

Tumbleweeds
www.tumbleweedquilts.com
1919 RT.6A
West Barnstable, MA 02668

Peaceful Quilting
www.piecefulquilting.com
4468 Middle Country Road
Calverton, NY 11933
and
3027 Jericho Turnpike
East Northport, NY 11731

City Quilter
www.cityquilter.com
133 West 25th Street
New York, NY 10001

Intown Quilters
www.intownquilters.com
1058 Mistletoe Road
Decatur, Georgia 30033

Thimbles
www.thimblesquilts.com
940 South State Street
Lockport, IL 60441

Mabel & Ethel's Quilt Shoppe
www.mequiltshoppe.com
279 E. Market Street
Sandusky, OH 44870

Fabric chain stores

Joann Fabrics and Crafts
www.joann.com/

Hancock Fabrics
www.hancockfabrics.com

Fabric suppliers

Andover Fabrics
www.andoverfabrics.com

Simplicity Creative Group
www.simplicity.com

Timeless Treasures
www.ttfabrics.com

Paper Pieces
www.paperpieces.com

Good books for further reading

Quilting on the Go
Jessica Alexandrakis (pub. 2013),
Potter Craft,
ISBN: 978-0770434120

All Points Patchwork
Diane Gilleland (pub. 2015),
Storey Publishing, LLC,
ISBN: 978-1612124209

First Steps to Free Motion Quilting
Christina Cameli (pub. 2013),
Stash Books,
ISBN: 978-1607056720

Step-by-Step Free Motion Quilting
Christina Cameli (pub. 2015),
Stash Books,
ISBN: 978-1617450242

Sunday Morning Quilts
Amanda Jean Nyberg and
Cheryl Arkison
(pub. 2012), C&T Publishing,
ISBN: 978-1607054276

Quilting with a Modern Slant
Rachel May (pub. 2014),
Storey Publishing, LLC,
ISBN: 978-1612120638

The Modern Quilt Workshop
Bill Kerr and Weeks Ringle
(pub. 2005), Quarry Books,
ISBN: 978-1592531523

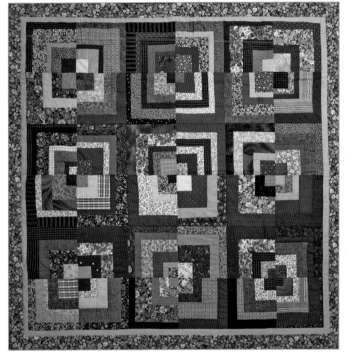

An example of "Improv Housetop,"
see page 116.

Index

Author Acknowledgements

Undergoing the process of writing a quilt book is a lot harder than making one, two, or even twenty quilts. I would not have been able to do it without the help and support of many people and I want to say thank you.

First, a big hug and kiss to Costas, George, and Jack. A quilter couldn't ask for a better family. I also need to express gratitude to everyone who helped take care of my children so I could have time to work on the book, most importantly Villy Alexandraki and Yamile Hurtado. And to my parents, I love you so much.

There are several quilters in my life who made writing this book a pleasure: Merrill Rosenberg, Shannon Couvillion, Helen Beall, Christa Farmer, Laura Catlan, Bernadette Forward, Eri Sakakibara, Kikuyo Kubota, Hayden Lees, and the rest of the NYC Mod Guild, along with countless friends on Instagram and blogs.

Hugs and thank yous to the team of quilters who helped stitch samples: Naomi Mankowitz, Merrill Rosenberg, Laura Catlan, and Gilma Simone. The quilters who lent quilts for photography: Shannon Couvillion, Shiobhan Toner, Karen Small, and Evelyne Wheeler.

And none of this would have been possible without the excellent team at Quarto: Kate Kirby, Lily de Gatacre, and Jackie Palmer. Plus my talented photographer, Ned Witrogen. Timeless Treasures Fabric, Andover Fabric, and Paperpieces.com generously donated materials for the projects and samples in this book, and I am grateful to have worked with such fantastic products and friendly people.

Credits

© 2015 Janome UK Ltd, p.19
Catlan, Laura, p.2
Couvillion, Shannon, pp.35t, 73
GAP Interiors/Dan Duchars, p.46
Jenkinson, Ruth, Getty Images, p.49
Mankowiz, Naomi, p.6bl, 119
Rosenberg, Merrill, pp.6tl, 55
Simone, Gilma, pp.6ctl/cbl, 109, 127
Small, Karen, p.157
Time Inc. (UK) Ltd, www.timeincukcontent.com, pp.15t, 29t
Toner, Siobhan, pp.25t, 106, 123
Wheeler, Evelyne, p.99